THE LEEDS, SETTLE
& CARLISLE RAI

C000254535

The Midland Route to Scotland

Martin Bairstow

4 – 6 – 2 No 70000 "Britannia" entering Garsdale with a Hellifield to Carlisle slow in July 1963. Built in 1951, the first of 999 BR "standard" locos, "Britannia" was withdrawn in 1966 but is preserved.
(Peter Sunderland)

Published by Martin Bairstow, 53 Kirklees Drive, Farsley, Leeds
Printed by The Amadeus Press, Cleckheaton West Yorkshire

Introduction

This is an enlarged and updated edition of a book which first appeared in 1994. There have been two principal developments since then. One was foreseen because electrification and re-signalling between Leeds and Skipton were already well in hand. The other came as a surprise, when heavy freight returned to the line.

The route from Leeds to Carlisle is 113 miles long. It was built in three parts, four if you count the short section of the North Eastern Railway, which is used for access into Carlisle. The first 26 miles from Leeds to Skipton were opened in 1846-47. This stretch is now electrified, carrying an intensive local passenger service along with longer distance diesel trains and heavy through freight. The next 14 miles to Settle Junction are part of the "Little" North Western Railway, which dates from 1849. The 72 miles from here to Petteril Bridge Junction, are the Settle & Carlisle line, fully opened in 1876.

There have been many books written about the Settle & Carlisle line but one masterpiece stands out above the rest; North of Leeds by Peter E Baughan, first published in 1966. The present book owes much to North of Leeds.

I am grateful to everyone else who has helped with the book. Peter Davies helped with the first chapter, John Holroyd with artwork and the sadly now late Geoffrey Lewthwaite with tickets. The photographs are credited individually.

Appreciation is also due to the many people who contributed to the fight to keep the line open. I have to confess that in the early 1980s, I thought the cause was hopeless. I am glad I was proved wrong.

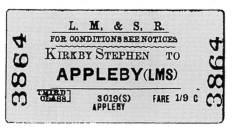

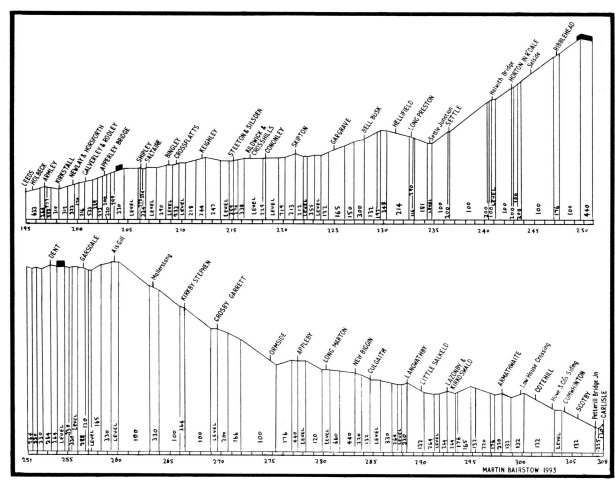

MARTIN BAIRSTOW 1993

A Journey from Leeds to Carlisle

"The Thames – Clyde Express" was the name introduced by the LMS in 1927 to distinguish the daytime
London – Glasgow service by the Midland route. The through journey time in 1938 was 8 hours 48 minutes.
"Royal Scot" class No 46113 "Cameronian" prepares to leave Leeds City on 11 May 1959.

(J C W Halliday)

The mile posts are counted from London St Pancras. It is always "up" to the zero mile post so it is "down" from Leeds to Carlisle and "up" coming back. The present mile posts date from 1914, prior to which the Settle & Carlisle line was measured from Settle Junction.

The first leg of the journey, the 11 miles from Leeds to Shipley, is completed in 12 minutes. Travellers may hardly notice it – even those who are journeying for the scenery. It just happens that this stretch of line is the one with which I was most familiar in the early 1960s before everything began to change out of recognition.

The Harrogate line diverges at Wortley Junction. Apart from the goods loops at Kirkstall, there are then just two plain tracks all the way to Shipley. Up until the 1960s, it was a quadruple track line with five intermediate stations, each with an attendant goods yard. There were private sidings at Kirkstall power station, at Kirkstall Forge and at Apperley Viaduct for Esholt Sewage Works. There were 14 signal boxes, including Armley Canal Road No 1 which stood on a gantry. Many of the block sections were so short that the outer and inner distants were positioned beneath the home and starter signals of the previous box. The

entire lineside was a forest of signals and telegraph poles.

The two pairs of tracks were designated "fast" and "slow". This had nothing to do with the speed of trains. The fast lines gave a direct run from Leeds to Bradford. They crossed over the slow by a flyover between Armley and Kirkstall. Leeds to Carlisle expresses normally used the slow lines.

The widening was carried out piecemeal over a number of years around 1900. The surviving pair of tracks are the former slow lines. They are on the original alignment on some stretches. Through Apperley Bridge Station, the slow lines were original but immediately beyond, the whole thing veers to the right putting the slow lines on new alignment and leaving the fast on the 1846 formation. From the down slow platform 3, you could see a train emerging from the fast line Thackley Tunnel nearly a mile away. It appeared to be coming straight towards you, but on the final approach, it would curve to the left and pass through platform 2.

The ten arch Apperley Viaduct is just one of eight crossings of the River Aire between Leeds and Shipley. The adjacent disused structure dates from

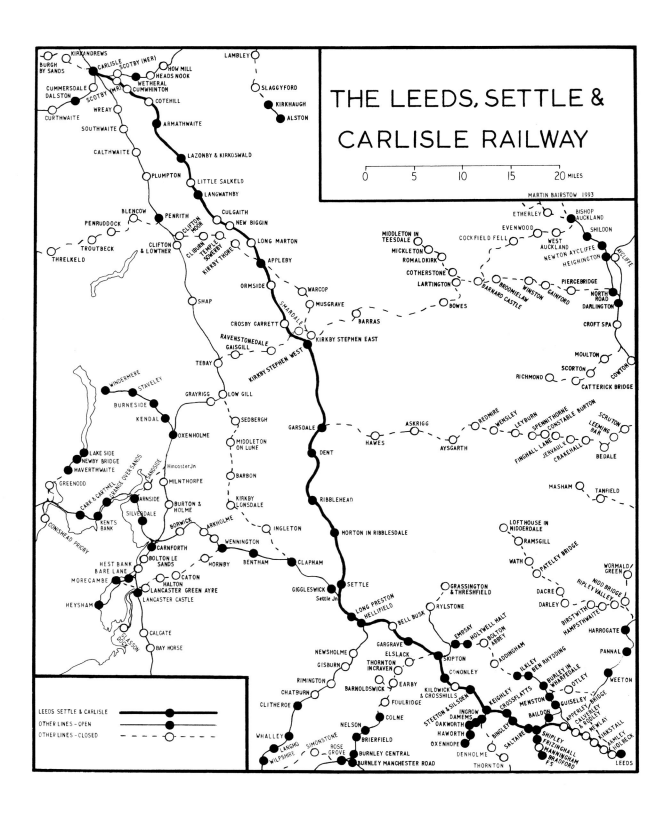

THE LEEDS, SETTLE &
CARLISLE RAILWAY

MARTIN BAIRSTOW 1993

LEEDS SETTLE & CARLISLE
OTHER LINES - OPEN
OTHER LINES - CLOSED

60069 "Sceptre" passing the closed station at Holbeck with the down "Thames Clyde Express" on 7 June 1961. *(G W Morrison)*

Approaching Kirkstall on 31 March 1961. The same A3 class 60069 "Sceptre" heads the 9.20am relief Glasgow St Enoch to London St Pancras, whilst 2 – 6 – 0 No 43117 has the 1.58pm Bradford F S to Birmingham on the up fast. *(David Holmes)*

1867, a replacement for the original which collapsed in a storm on 14 November 1866. There are also four bridges over the Leeds & Liverpool Canal.

The original 1,496 yard Thackley Tunnel was straight for more than half its length, with a curve at the Shipley end. The present 1900 tunnel is on the outside of the curve and slightly longer at 1,518 yards.

Approaching Shipley, just before the Bradford line diverges, the building on the left is the former Great Northern station, terminus of the branch from Bradford Exchange via Idle. It closed as long ago as 1931.

Prior to 1979, there was no main line platform at Shipley. Historically, there had been sufficient trains into Bradford to give Shipley a comprehensive service but most of these were withdrawn in 1965 after which Leeds to Skipton trains performed a setting back manoeuvre. The down main line platform, the present No 2, was built in 1979 and signalled for reversible working the following year. The up platform was commissioned in 1992.

Saltaire is the model village built around Titus Salt's Mill in the 1850s. The station had low platforms prior to closure in 1965. It reopened in 1984. Nearby is the short cable worked Shipley Glen Tramway.

Bingley Station dates from 1892. Its predecessor was a little further on by the Three Rise Lock on the canal. The unique Five Rise Lock is also visible from the train.

The Midland Railway resisted requests for a station at Crossflatts, claiming it was too near Bingley, but the West Yorkshire PTE thought differently and provided one in 1982. Crossflatts was the furthest extent of the 4ft gauge Bradford City Tramways which reached there in 1914, but closed in 1939.

The railway from Shipley to Skipton was never quadrupled throughout but there were goods lines on the outside of the passenger lines from Bingley to Thwaites and again for the last mile and a half from Snaygill into Skipton.

Keighley Station was built in its present position in 1883, with diverging platforms for the Worth Valley branch and the Great Northern lines from Bradford and Halifax via Queensbury. The latter closed to passengers in 1955 and to goods a year later. The Worth Valley line was also discarded in 1962 but after six years it came back to life courtesy of the Keighley & Worth Valley Railway Preservation Society. It operates both steam and diesel services at weekends throughout the year and daily in summer. Keighley Station is unique in this country in having steam, diesel and electric trains on regular timetabled service.

On the freight side, Keighley was the last Aire Valley station to lose its goods facility in 1981. The site is now a supermarket which has had the effect of pulling the focal point of the town towards the station.

Keighley Station Junction box dating from 1884 stands disused just beyond the bridge. Its operational position was a little further on by the zero milepost for the Worth Valley branch, which is still in place.

The three intermediate stations between Keighley and Skipton all closed in 1965 but Steeton & Silsden and Cononley reopened in 1990 and 1988 respectively. Kildwick & Crosshills remains closed. It was originally on the Skipton side of the level crossing, where the original building still stands. This served as the station master's house when the station itself moved to the far side of the next road bridge in 1889.

As the train curves into Skipton, it passes under the viaduct built for the Ilkley line in 1888. This still carries freight from the quarry at Rylstone on the truncated Grassington branch.

Skipton Station moved to its present site on 1 May 1876, the day the Settle & Carlisle line opened to passengers. There were four platforms in the main station, to which two were added at a slightly higher level when the Ilkley line opened in 1888. Skipton declined in importance with closure of the lines to

Of the former stations between Leeds and Shipley, the most tangible remain is the road level building at Armley Canal Road. Unseen by rail travellers, the bricked up passage on the right used to lead down to the platforms. *(Martin Bairstow)*

A Hudswell Clarke 0 – 4 – 0ST at Kirkstall Power Station in 1965. Commissioned in 1931, the station was on the north side, close to the fast line flyover. It closed in 1976.

(John Holroyd)

Kirkstall Station, newly rebuilt with four platforms, looking towards Leeds in 1905.

(Martin Bairstow collection)

An early view of Newlay, looking towards Leeds. The station is a few yards nearer Bradford than the later structure, the main building standing between the bridge over the river and the level crossing, which was later replaced by the road bridge. There appears to be a signal box behind the double arm signal.

(Martin Bairstow collection)

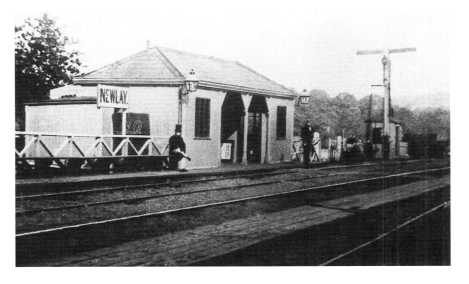

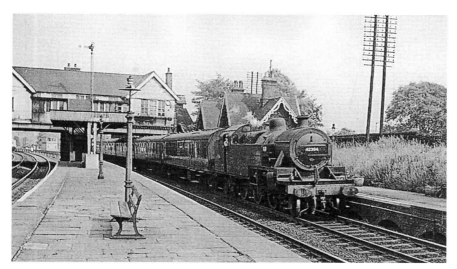

2 – 6 – 4T No 42394 passing Calverley & Rodley on 28 June 1964 with an express from London St Pancras to Bradford Forster Square. The tank engine had come on at Leeds. The Settle & Carlisle type structure on the down fast platform was the main building until quadrupling around 1900.

(Ben Brooksbank)

The pre 1900 station at Apperley Bridge, looking towards Shipley. The overall roof, main building and down platform were swept away when the cutting was widened for the additional pair of tracks. The up platform survived until 1965.

(Stuart Carmichael)

An up freight passing through Apperley Bridge on the "slow" line. The station existed in this form from the quadrupling around 1900 until closure in 1965.

(Martin Bairstow collection)

Midland 4F 0 – 6 – 0 No 43987 approaching Apperley Bridge with a northbound freight on 10 July 1956. The train is on the "fast" line now lifted. The "slow" lines are to the left and the Ilkley branch on the ledge.

(J C W Halliday)

Sister engine No 43871 has just passed Apperley Bridge with a freight on the down slow on 21 July 1955.

(J C W Halliday)

From the 1920s, until the early 1970s, Esholt Sewage Works had an extensive private system with an exchange siding at Apperley Viaduct. 0 – 4 – 0ST "Nellie" crossing the Leeds & Liverpool Canal in March 1969.
(John Holroyd)

333 005 calls at Shipley with a Skipton to Leeds working on 26 May 2012. *(Martin Bairstow)*

Just off the Leeds – Carlisle route, south of Shipley Station, Crossley's scrap yard still dispatches traffic by rail. One of their present shunters is 0 – 4 – 0 diesel "Prince of Wales", built for Esholt Sewage Works in 1969. On 27 July 1984, they were using Andrew Barclay 0 – 4 – 0ST "Harry".
(John Holroyd)

48423 rounding Shipley curve with northbound coal about 1965. The two distant signals offer fast and slow lines towards Leeds. This is now the location of the main line platforms.

(Martin Bairstow collection)

Ilkley in 1965 and Colne in 1970. The latter closure was particularly vindictive, severing a through route by removing 12 miles in the middle. The station was reduced to just the through platforms 2 and 3 but 1 and 4 were reopened as part of the electrification scheme.

Beyond the station is the electric train depot on the right. The former steam shed was on the other side, where there is now an industrial estate. Beyond here, the line to Settle curves to the right. This is Skipton North Junction, where the Colne line used to diverge straight ahead.

Only a few Carlisle trains stop at Gargrave, where part of the "Little North Western" building remains as a private house. The original stone shelter survives on the down platform. The River Aire is crossed for the last time just before Bell Busk, which closed in 1959. The platforms have long been removed but the main building survives as a guest house.

The summit of the "Little" North Western is reached a mile and a half before Hellifield. This is the watershed between the River Aire which flows east and the Ribble which flows into the Irish Sea.

The village of Hellifield was transformed into a small town when the railway became a junction in 1880. The original "Little" North Western station was half a mile before the present one and would have been convenient for the new houses which have appeared in recent years.

The present station opened in 1880 for interchange between the Midland and Lancashire & Yorkshire Railways. Comprising a long island platform with bays at each end, its size is out of proportion to any indigenous traffic it was likely to generate. Today, the trains stop at the Leeds extremity. The remainder was a decaying ruin until renovation in the 1990s.

Goods loops still run on the outside of the passenger lines. The layout is controlled with semaphore signals by Hellifield South Junction which fringes on to York power box. From here to the outskirts of Carlisle, the route is on manual signalling with modern adaptations.

The engine shed used to be on the up side, at the Carlisle end of the station.

The half finished shed and approach road on the down side are part of a project which collapsed in the 1990s

Long Preston has lost all its original buildings. Crude bus shelters afford protection from the elements. It compares most unfavourably with the unstaffed stations on the Settle & Carlisle line itself.

The splitting home signal at Settle Junction confirms that we are the main line. The arm for Carlisle is higher than the one for the Morecambe line, which has been subject to a 15mph limit with a single turnout ever since a parcels train derailed and damaged the junction in 1979. Opposite the 1913 signal box, there stood until the 1960s, the remains of the short lived Settle Junction Station.

Settle Junction is the start of the "long drag", so

"Black Five" No 45466 pilots a "Jubilee" round the main line curve at Shipley in September 1958. *(Peter Sunderland)*

Opened in 1856 to serve Titus Salt's model village, Saltaire Station closed on 20 March 1965. It reopened on the same site on 9 April 1984. 31445 passes with the 11.05 Hull – Lancaster on 23 June that year. *(Tom Heavyside)*

called by generations of firemen who faced an almost unbroken climb at 1 in 100 for the next 15 miles. The green dome of Giggleswick School is visible to the west from Settle Station.

This is built in stone in the gothic style which characterises all but one of the stations on the route. There are three sizes; small medium and large. Settle is one of the last named variety. Passengers enter by a side gate, not though the main building which has no rear entrance. There is a waiting room on the other platform which was reached only by a foot crossing until 1993 when the footbridge was installed. This came from Drem on the East Coast Main Line.

In Midland tradition, the station master's house was not an integral part of the station but a detached house, which has been sold off and modernised. The water tower has also been converted into a residence. The signal box, closed in 1984, has been restored as a demonstration box which can normally be visited on Saturdays.

In the days when the Station Master lived on the premises and had plenty of staff, he could tend the station gardens. This service is no longer available from the full time staff but the Settle & Carlisle line has pioneered the involvement of volunteers. The "heritage" lighting was commissioned in the late 1990s and is standard for all the Settle & Carlisle line stations. The altitude and distance signs are based on a similar display created by Station Master Taylor in the early 1960s. He persuaded BR to stop the "Thames-Clyde" and other expresses at Settle rather than Hellifield. Without this, Settle might have closed with the other local stations in 1970.

Two viaducts are needed to carry the line out of Settle. Marshfield of four arches is followed by Settle Viaduct of six. A mile further on was the Craven Lime Company's siding at Stainforth. After the short Staincliffe Tunnel, there are two more viaducts, Little and Sheriff Brow, each of three arches and both crossing the Ribble in what has now become a narrow valley between Moughton Fell on the left and Fountains Fell on the right.

At Helwith Bridge, there used to be an inclined railway bringing stone from a quarry on Moughton Fell down to the exchange sidings. We cross the Ribble again by the five arch Ribble Bridge Viaduct.

On the approach to Horton in Ribblesdale, we pass the site of extensive quarries, whose sidings used to trail in on the left just before the station. The signal box closed in 1984. Its function after the sidings had gone was to split the block section. That is now achieved by the intermediate home and distant signals, which are worked from the box in arrear – Settle Junction in the down direction, Blea Moor in the up.

The original buildings survive on both platforms. Once derelict, they have been brought back into use,

making this a complete example of one of the small stations. Though unstaffed, it is well maintained by volunteers. The altitude sign replicates the one created by Station Master Taylor in the 1950s, before he moved to Settle. Behind is the detached house where he lived. Beyond that, the scene is dominated by Penyghent.

Horton in Ribblesdale is where keen walkers alight to attempt the Three Peaks embracing Penyghent (2,273 ft), Whernside (2,414 ft) and Ingelborough (2,372 ft). The total distance is 24 miles and requires 4,750 feet of ascent. Walkers should set out on the expedition well equipped.

With Ingleborough ahead on the left and Penyghent just two miles away to the right, the railway sets a fairy straight course through the hamlet of Selside which is passed on an embankment. There

Ex LNWR "Claughton" 4 – 6 – 0 No 5932 "Sir Thomas Williams" with a southbound express east of Bingley. Twenty of these locos were transferred to Holbeck and Durran Hill Sheds in 1927, bringing heavier motive power to the Leeds – Carlisle route than had been afforded by the Midland.
(W Hubert Foster, courtesy John Holroyd)

Horse drawn cabs outside Bingley Station. The external awnings were removed in the 1960s.
(Martin Bairstow collection)

42928 approaching Bingley with an up stopping train on 3 August 1955. *(Gordon Coltas)*

46145 "The Duke of Wellington's Regiment" passing Marley Junction with the down "Waverley" on 31 July 1960. Marley Junction was just a series of cross overs on the four track Bingley to Thwaites section.

(Martin Bairstow collection)

Keighley is one of very few stations where you can see steam, diesel and electric trains at the same time, all on timetabled service. Then recently preserved class 108 DMU, Nos 50928 and 51568 await departure for Oxenhope on 29 May 1993.

(Martin Bairstow)

"Royal Scot" 4 – 6 – 0 No 46108 "Seaforth Highlander" passing non stop through Keighley with the up "Thames Clyde" in June 1957.
(Peter Sunderland)

was a signal box here until 1975 but requests for a station never met with success. The signal box is "preserved" at Carnforth in dilapidated condition.

On the right, a mile short of Ribblehead, are Salt Lake Cottages, opposite the one time Salt Lake Quarry which provided some of the stone for Ribblehead Viaduct. All along the route are examples of cottages which the Railway built to house workers

Ribblehead is a remote spot comprising little more than the station and a pub. In 1938, the station master was appointed by the Meteorological Office to send hourly weather reports, an arrangement which continued until the station became unstaffed at the beginning of 1967.

The down platform was removed in 1974 to make way for a new siding which was used for loading stone quarried near Ingleton and brought there by road. For a brief time this traffic, largely for use as railway ballast, filled two trains a day but by 1986 it had stopped. When the station reopened, it was served in the up direction only until the new platform was commissioned in May 1993.

A little way beyond the station the line singles. This was done in 1984 to allow the track to be slewed into the centre of Ribblehead Viaduct to spread the weight. Whether his was done for structural or political reasons is open to question. Under the shadow of Whernside, the 24 arches carry the line a maximum of 165 feet above the ground. Every sixth pier is of additional strength. This has the visual effect of dividing the quarter mile structure into four equal lengths.

Blea Moor is very remote. Even today, when most signalmen have cars, the last mile must be covered on foot. Yet there is demand to work there. As manual boxes close elsewhere, the Settle & Carlisle provides an opportunity for signalmen who wish to remain in

this type of work. The derelict cottage used to be part of a group housing railway staff at this lonely outpost.

The box replaced one of Midland design on the other side of the line. It was commissioned in 1941 when the up and down refuge sidings were upgraded into loops. Previously, if a slow freight needed to be overtaken, it had to set back into the siding. This time consuming manoeuvre avoided having facing points on the main line but was incompatible with wartime pressures.

In Midland days, there was only one facing point on the entire Settle & Carlisle line. In the normal direction of travel, trains would never face a choice of route. If, exceptionally, a passenger train had to reverse over what was normally a trailing point, then this would have to be clamped by hand.

The down loop was removed in January 1985, when the track over Ribblehead Viaduct was singled. The up loop is still in use, allowing freight trains to be held before negotiating the single track bottleneck.

Beyond Blea Moor, the line enters a cutting before plunging into the 2,629 yard tunnel. The "Long Drag" ends just inside giving way to a gentle down grade. There are three ventilation shafts, each ten feet in diameter. The deepest one, nearest the northern end has a depth of 390 feet. Emerging from the tunnel, there follows what many travellers consider the most spectacular two miles of the journey as the railway is carried on the hillside high above Dentdale. Dent Head Viaduct of ten arches carries the railway 100 feet over Fell End Gill. It then continues on a ledge into Great Knouterry Hill until this is broken by Arten Gill which the railway spans by an eleven arch viaduct.

A further mile and the train reaches Dent Station. The main building has been converted to holiday accommodation, as have the snow huts just to

Steeton & Silsden looking towards Leeds. The pre 1888 station was beyond the level crossing.
(Martin Bairstow collection)

47440 passing Cononley with a Carlisle to Leeds train shortly after the station reopened in 1988. *(Martin Bairstow)*

"Standard" 4 – 6 – 2 No 72009 "Clan Stewart" leaving Skipton with the afternoon Carlisle – Bradford slow. The last coach has just passed the pre 1876 station. *(Peter Sunderland)*

the south. The southbound waiting room has been restored and a new shelter provided on the northbound side. A board announces that this is the highest main line station in England, 1,150 feet above sea level. It is also one of the remotest as the village is over four miles away. The former station master's house is the only other sign of life nearby.

After going under the four arch bridge carrying the Garsdale to Dent "coal road", the railway passes through a cutting before entering the 1,213 yard Rise Hill Tunnel which is level throughout.

The line emerges on a ledge overlooking Garsdale. It was on this level section that the Midland built the water troughs in 1907. They were 557 yards long, each holding over 5,000 gallons of water of which some 2,000 gallons could be scooped up by a thirsty locomotive.

Apart from the railway cottages, Garsdale is three miles from the nearest settlement. Originally called Hawes Junction, it was built primarily for interchange. The station was in compatible style to others on the line but with no main building. There is the usual shelter on the northbound side. The ticket office was incorporated in the similar but larger structure on the island platform which served both the up main line

and the Hawes branch. There was no direct access from the main line on to the Hawes branch. Any movement involved reversing over trailing points.

The signal box on the down platform dates from 1910, when it replaced the separate north and south boxes. From 1983, it was normally switched out except in emergencies. It reopened permanently with the resumption of freight traffic.

Prior to 1939, Garsdale had a small engine shed for the North Eastern loco working the Northallerton service. The turntable was stockaded to protect it from the weather. It remained derelict for many years until moved to Keighley where it was restored to working order in 1989. One of its functions in Midland days was to turn pilot engines which had assisted trains from either Hellifield or Carlisle and wished to go back facing boiler first.

The large water tower at the south end of the station doubled up as a social centre for local railwaymen and farmers whilst the waiting room served as a church and library.

Leaving Garsdale, the line curves to the left and crosses the 12 arch Dandry Mire Viaduct. The track bed of the Hawes branch can be seen disappearing to

Midland compound 4 – 4 – 0 No 1000 was built in 1902 and withdrawn in 1951. It was then restored for occasional use on special trains. It is seen arriving at Skipton on 4 September 1960, bound for Ravenglass.
(Peter Sunderland)

8F 2 – 8 – 0 No 48384 passing Skipton with up coal empties in June 1967. The Leeds – Settle – Carlisle route saw steam right up to August 1968.   *(Martin Bairstow)*

The driving trailer brings up the rear of a mark 4 electric being diesel hauled back towards Leeds on 11 June 1990. The overgrown Ilkley line platforms once had canopies.   *(Martin Bairstow)*

D144 crossing the River Aire between Gargrave and Skipton with the up "Thames – Clyde" on 28 March 1965.
(Martin Bairstow collection)

4 – 6 – 2 No 72008 "Clan MacLeod" passing Gargrave with an up relief train in July 1963.   *(Peter Sunderland)*

Midland 2P 4 – 4 – 0 No 40459 piloting "Black Five" No 45009 through Bell Busk about 1949.
(W Hubert Foster, courtesy John Holroyd)

the right. Then, beyond the 98 yard Moorcock Tunnel, comes Lunds Viaduct with five arches. Another short tunnel at Shotlock Hill, 106 yards brings the line alongside the Hawes to Kirkby Stephen road.

A further mile and the summit of the line is reached at Ais Gill, 1,169 feet above sea level. This is another lonely settlement with just a few cottages. The refuge sidings and signal box have been removed. The view ahead to the left is dominated by Wild Boar Fell as the train begins the descent at 1 in 100 and crosses Ais Gill Viaduct. The stream on the right is the River Eden which the railway now follows all the way to Carlisle where it flows into the Solway Firth.

The valley drops much more steeply than the railway which soon gains a commanding view across Mallerstang. There used to be goods loops and a signal box high above the village of Mallerstang but never a station as the Midland Railway insisted that somebody else would have to finance an access road. From the right of the train, a path can be seen on the hillside. This was the route used by Lady Ann Clifford in the seventeenth century from Castle Bolton in Wensleydale to her estate in the Eden Valley, which included Pendragon Castle, near Kirkby Stephen, Appleby Castle and Brougham near Penrith.

Beyond Mallerstang is Outhgill which boasts the smallest church in Cumbria. Faraday, the inventor of electricity was born in this village. The train enters a deep cutting before Birkett Tunnel, but if you are quick you may just catch a glimpse of Pendragon Castle. The fells beyond are those of High Pike Hill and High Seat, collectively known as Mallerstang Edge, forming a magnificent fell walk from Garsdale to Kirkby Stephen for the well shod walker.

Entering Birkett Tunnel, the train crosses the Pennine Fault. During construction no less than seven different minerals were encountered including coal. Beyond the tunnel, the red sandstone of the Eden Valley begins to dominate. Nine Standards Rigg is to the right. There are nine cairns on the summit which were built as boundary markers to denote the limit of the North Riding of Yorkshire.

Kirkby Stephen station stands 1½ miles from the town centre at the top of a hill. The standard Midland answer to an inconvenient station was to lengthen the name so their's became Kirkby Stephen & Ravenstonedale in honour of a small village 3½ miles to the west. British Railways tried Kirkby Stephen West for the Midland station and East for the North Eastern. Far West and Mid West would have been more accurate.

Traffic on the road from town to station is both heavy and fast moving. The road has no footpath. Finally, in July 2011, a surfaced path was opened away from the road for pedestrians and cyclists. The main building was converted into holiday accommodation in 2012. The footbridge was installed in 1999, having previously been at Guiseley. The BR pattern flat roof signal box was commissioned in 1974 to replace the Midland box dating from 1894. It utilised parts recovered from Kendal, where the box had closed the previous year.

Down below on the main road, the erstwhile social order is remembered with the detached house for the station master and row of six cottages for other grades.

The next major structure is the 12 arch Smardale Viaduct which crosses a beck 130 feet below. If you look up, you should get a glimpse on the left hand side of the northern end of Howgill Fells. Look down and you will see the track bed of the North Eastern

LNER 4 – 6 – 2 No 25 "Falcon" approaching Bell Busk on 12 August 1948 with the "Flying Scotsman", diverted because the East Coast Main Line was flooded in south east Scotland.

(W Hubert Foster, courtesy John Holroyd)

branch from Kirkby Stephen to Tebay, whose own Smardale Gill Viaduct can be glimpsed momentarily.

Views now open out to the west across the fertile Vale of Eden. The Lakeland Fells can be seen extending from Coniston Old man in the south to Blencathra in the north. Travellers familiar with the Lake District may recognise other fells, notably High Street with the outline of Helvellyn just behind.

Crosby Garrett Tunnel (181 yards) leads on to the six arch viaduct which carries the line above the village. The church can be seen on the right standing on elevated ground. As at Smardale and Ormside, it was built on higher ground as a defence against possible invasion from north of the border.

Crosby Garrett Station, closed in 1953 was in a cutting. Up and down platform shelters were set into recesses, the retaining walls for which are still visible. The main building was at the north end of the up platform. The station master's house can still be seen over to the right.

Two miles further on, the line is carried over Potts Beck by the seven arch Griseburn Viaduct. This is closely followed on the left by the site of Griseburn Ballast Sidings, which had a signal box on the down side from 1905 until 1981. Beyond Helm Tunnel (571 yards), views open out on the east side towards Stainmore and the brooding frame of Mickle Fell, the highest peak in Yorkshire.

Ormside closed as long ago as 1952 but the main building and station master's house are still there on the down side, the first ones to appear in red sandstone. Hitherto, the buildings have been in grey Yorkshire stone.

The River Eden is crossed for the first time by Ormside Viaduct which numbers ten arches. On the approach to Appleby, the Stainmore (Darlington to Penrith) lines comes into view. Closed as a through route in 1962, the five miles between Warcop and Appleby remained in use for army traffic until 1989. The track is still in place and there is an attempt to reopen it as a heritage railway.

Appleby goods yard is now a heritage centre which is more of a workshop facility than a museum. Outside stands 4 – 6 – 0 No 4979 "Wootton Hall" which hasn't run since 1963. It passed via Barry scrapyard from where it was rescued from scrap but still awaits a realistic prospect of restoration.

The buildings at Appleby are brick with sandstone dressings. The footbridge dates from 1901 and was for over 90 years the only one on the Settle & Carlisle line.

Appleby North box is a 1951 replacement for one which burnt down. It is so called to distinguish from Appleby Station box, which closed in 1973. It controls the now rarely used double track junction onto the North Eastern. In Midland days, this was the only facing point on the Settle & Carlisle line. It had to be because there was once a passenger service from Appleby (Midland) to Penrith.

The North Eastern used to pass under the Midland, about the same spot where the bypass goes under now. The views from the right of the train are of Murten Fell and Pike, with a glimpse of High Cup Nick. As the train continues, Knock Old Man is revealed with the highest weather station in England on Great Dunn Fell, visible just beyond Little Dunn Fell. The eye then perceives the outline of Cross Fell, the highest point in the Pennines and summit of the Pennine Way National Trail.

The run down to Long Marton includes a viaduct

2 – 4 – 0 No 1402 at Hellifield with a train of six wheelers. Built at Derby in 1879, No 1402 was part of a batch of ten locos allocated to Lancaster and Carnforth for use on the "Little" North Western route.
(W Hubert Foster, courtesy John Holroyd)

"Black Five" No 45481 with a down passenger train at Appleby on 22 August 1964. It is about to negotiate what was historically the only facing point on the route.

(Peter E Baughan)

Hellifield North Junction.box, which closed in March 1966. Engine shed to left.

(W Hubert Foster, courtesy John Holroyd)

Hellifield looking north towards the loco shed. The boy porter takes a well earned rest.

(G Lambert collection)

2 – 6 – 4T No 42492 stands in the bay at Hellifield on 10 January 1959, ready to depart with the afternoon local to Hawes.

(J C W Halliday)

45109 entering Long Preston with the 11.58 Hellifield to Carlisle stopper on 19 March 1965.

(Peter E Baughan)

of five arches carrying the line 60 feet above Trout Beck. The station building on the up side now serves as holiday accommodation. The Station Master's house is on the down side.

The gypsum mine at Kirkby Thore was a long standing source of rail traffic but it ceased before the run down. In 1993, it led the freight revival. Access is controlled by a signal box which looks like two portakabins, one on top of the other.

The next closed station, New Biggin, has been converted to a private house with a conservatory at one end. New Biggin Viaduct of four arches crosses Crowdundle Beck which flows into the Eden a little way to the west.

Culgaith is another closed station whose main building has been converted into a private house. It was built four years after the others in totally different style. The level crossing, the first since Cononley, has ensured survival of the 1908 signal box. A short way beyond, the line negotiates two tunnels: Culgaith (661 yards) and Waste Bank (164 yards). The River Eamont, which has flowed out of Ullswater, can be seen joining the Eden about a mile further on the left.

The main building at Langwathby is the Brief Encounter Restaurant, which opened in 1996. There are replacement shelters on both platforms. Langwathby is the nearest point to the Lake District and here, one feels, is a missed opportunity for a bus connection.

Little Salkeld or Dodd's Mill Viaduct of seven arches crosses Briggles Beck. The closed station at Little Salkeld remains substantially intact, including the platforms. The main building is a private residence.

On the east side beyond Little Salkeld is a small hill on top of which are the remains of a Druids' Temple, known as "Long Meg and her Daughters" "Long Meg" is a square stone, 18 feet high and 15 feet in girth with four corners coinciding with the main points of the compass. The "Daughters" are 66 smaller stones arranged in a circle.

A BR pattern signal box with flat roof stands derelict at Long Meg Sidings. Commissioned in 1955, it was closed in 1983. The quarry produced rail traffic on and off from 1896 until 1976. The quarry's last steam locomotive, 0 – 4 – 0ST "W S T" (meaning William Steuart Trimble) is preserved at the Bowes Railway.

The original Long Meg signal box closed in 1915. For the next 40 years there was only a ground frame connecting on to the up line but an upsurge in traffic required full block facilities. The River Eden passes under the seven arch Eden Lacy Viaduct and remains on the east side of the line for the remainder of the journey.

Lazonby has witnessed some population growth with new houses near to the station. The main building serves as offices for Bells of Lazonby whose bakery business occupies the goods yard. The building is well maintained, with its Potts clock showing the correct time. But it is inaccessible to passengers who must rely on a bus shelter, the first since Long Preston. Those in the southbound direction have the authentic Midland waiting room. Kirkoswald, the other half of the station name, lies 1¼ miles to the north east on the far side of the Eden.

Between Lazonby and Armathwaite, the river passes through the Eden Gorge. Views from the train are intermittent because of the trees. Three tunnels follow in quick succession: Baron Wood No 1 (207 yards), Baron Wood No 2 (251 yards) and Armathwaite (325 yards).

The valley widens beyond the gorge. The railway curves to the right crossing the nine arch Armathwaite Viaduct. Armathwaite Station stands some way above the village which is close by the river. The main building is well restored as a private house. It fronts onto the down platform without any of the fortifications mentioned in the 1994 edition. Again it's a bus shelter for Carlisle but a Midland waiting room for Leeds.

The signal box dating from 1899 was closed in 1983. BR threatened demolition but in 1992 it was restored by the Friends of the Settle - Carlisle line and painted in Midland livery.

Cold Fell rises to the right beyond Armathwaite. This marks the northern limit of the Pennine Range before the ground descends to the Newcastle – Carlisle gap.

In the remaining ten miles to Carlisle, there were three stations which in Midland days ranked amongst the best used in terms of passenger numbers. Yet they were amongst the first to close because their short distance traffic into Carlisle was the easiest prey to bus competition.

Having traversed the seven arch Drybeck Viaduct, the line curves to the west on a high embankment. Low House Crossing retains its Midland signal box of 1900. The quarter mile long Eden Brow embankment leads to the four arch High Stand Gill Viaduct. Little evidence remains that there was a station at Cotehill, apart from a row of terraced railway cottages on what used to be the approach road. Howe & Cos Siding is the fringe box for Carlisle power box. The name recalls the steeply graded siding, which used to serve the alabaster works, ¾ mile to the south west. It closed about 1980. Two 0 – 4 – 0STs "John Howe" and "J N Derbyshire" are preserved at the Ribble Steam Railway, Preston.

Despite closure in 1956, Cumwhinton Station is remarkably well preserved with platforms and buildings in tact on both sides. The main building and station Master's house survive at Scotby, which closed in 1942. This village also had a station on the Newcastle line but this closed in 1959.

By the time it passes under the motorway, the train has almost completed its descent. The Newcastle line appears on the right. We run parallel for a further mile before joining it at Petteril Bridge Junction, named after the river we cross immediately beyond.

"Jubilee" class 4 – 6 – 0 No 45566 "Queensland" passing Long Preston on Whit Tuesday 1958 with the 9am relief from Glasgow St Enoch to Leeds. *(Peter Sunderland)*

The Midland engine shed was at Durran Hill on the left just before the Junction.

At London Road Junction, a sharply curved single track branches off to join the West Coast Main Line. Then a double track leaves to join the Whitehaven line. At which point the combined Settle and Newcastle lines reduce to a single track for the final approach into Carlisle. The second track is still in place as an electrified siding.

Carlisle Citadel dates from 1847, when it became the joint station of the Lancaster & Carlisle and Caledonian Railways. It was enlarged in 1863 and 1880 to accommodate all the railways terminating in Carlisle. The second rebuilding was part financed by the Midland to accommodate Settle & Carlisle business. The work could not begin until through goods traffic had been diverted on to the avoiding line which opened in 1877. This closed on 1 May 1984, when a northbound freightliner derailed causing damage which was never repaired. Through freight now has to go via the station again.

Before the 1923 Grouping, Carlisle Citadel was used by seven companies, four English and three Scottish. Only the North British with its Silloth Branch and Waverley Route to Edinburgh has closed. Descendants of the other six are still present. The Citadel suffix is optional. There hasn't been any other Carlisle Station since 1863. The station has eight platforms. Nos 1, 3 and 4 are through. No 2 is the Whitehaven bay, whilst 5 and 6 are bays for Leeds and Newcastle. Nos 7 and 8 are bays for the Glasgow & South Western.

The high retaining walls are a relic of the overall roof which spanned both the passenger station and the carriage sidings. Dating from the 1880 rebuilding, it was demolished in 1957 and replaced by a much smaller roof with canopies on some of the newly exposed platforms.

The remains of Settle Junction Station, opposite the signal box, in 1964. It opened on 1 November 1876, intended to replace Settle (Old) but the latter continued as Giggleswick and the Junction Station closed on 31 October 1877.
(Peter E Baughan)

D1855 approaching Settle Junction with a diverted Glasgow to Manchester service on Sunday 15 May 1966.
(Martin Bairstow collection)

The 1913 signal box at Settle Junction still controls the divergence of the Carlisle and Morecambe lines. "Standard" 4 – 6 – 0 No 75015 is probably delivering coal for the box on 15 May 1966.
(Martin Bairstow collection)

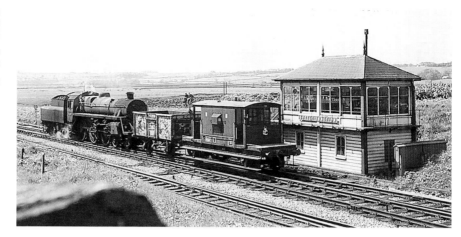

158794 is framed in the former Drem footbridge at Settle on 28 April 2012.

(Martin Bairstow)

The altitude sign at Settle, the work of Station Master James Taylor, in 1963.

(Peter E Baughan)

"Black Five" No 45109 taking water at Settle Station on 19 March 1965, whilst working the 11.58am stopper from Hellifield to Carlisle. *(Peter E Baughan)*

47407 crossing Sheriff Brow Viaduct with the 10.45 from Leeds on 25 August 1989. *(David A Smith)*

The Midland Route to Scotland

The Railway opened as far as Stainforth Sidings in 1873. The 1898 signal box was replaced in 1950 and abolished in 1963. View looking north about 1946. *(W Hubert Foster, courtesy John Holroyd)*

The railway from Settle Junction to Carlisle was conceived and built for one purpose only – as a main line to Scotland. It was engineered for fast running. The intention was to create a Midland alternative to the East and West Coast Main Lines. Intermediate traffic was a minor consideration. There was very little potential anyway.

Before going on to consider the main subject of the book, we must look at the origins of the Midland Railway and its ambition to become an Anglo Scottish main line.

Hudson's Derby Empire

The Midland Railway was formed in 1844 by the amalgamation of three railways converging on Derby; the Midland Counties, the Derby & Birmingham Junction and the North Midland. The last named had extended from Rotherham to Leeds on 1 July 1840, placing that City on a continuous railway from London. The route was by what is now the West Coast Main Line from Euston to Rugby, then the Midland Counties and North Midland via Derby.

At the time of its formation, the Midland was the Country's largest railway. Its Chairman was George Hudson, the "Railway King" whose rise and fall is summarised in *Railways in East Yorkshire Volume One.* For a period of four years, the Midland headquarters at Derby was one of Hudson's main power bases. The Railway Mania was in full swing.

By the early twentieth century, the Midland had reached the South Coast near Bournemouth and the Essex Coast at Southend. Its tentacles spread into South Wales. It had an extensive system in Ireland and a share in the Forth Bridge. It was the third largest railway, immediately prior to the 1923 "Grouping".

The Leeds & Bradford Railway

This enterprise is described more fully in *Railways Through Airedale & Wharfedale*. The 13½ mile route was authorised in 1844. It opened on 30 June 1846, just a few days after it had been leased to the Midland. The circumstances of this lease turned out to be a factor in the downfall of George Hudson.

Meanwhile the Leeds & Bradford Extension Railway had been authorised in 1845. This was also covered by the Midland lease. It opened from Shipley to Keighley in March 1847 and to Skipton six months later. After that it headed to Colne where from 1849 it made end on connection with the East Lancashire Railway.

The Leeds & Bradford built its own passenger terminus at Wellington Station in Leeds. Other Midland traffic was transferred from the less convenient Hunslet Lane. The site of Wellington is roughly platforms 1 to 5 of the present station plus the car park.

The Lancaster & Carlisle Railway

This undertaking built 69 miles of what became the West Coast Main Line. It was promoted in 1844, with financial backing from the four companies, the London & Birmingham, Grand Junction, North Union and Preston & Lancaster Junction, which had brought the railway as far north as Lancaster. On 16 July 1846, these were amalgamated to form the London & North Western Railway.

Despite the difficult territory which had to be negotiated, the line was built quickly, opening through to Carlisle on 15 February 1848. Traffic was worked by the LNWR until August 1857 when the Lancaster & Carlisle assumed responsibility. This period of independence lasted only two years. Towards the end of 1859, the LNWR took fright that the L&C might fall to the Midland. So they agreed a 999 year lease which guaranteed L&C shareholders an 8% dividend. The LNWR itself paid only 4%.

The "Little" North Western Railway

Incorporated on 26 June 1846, the prefix was unofficial to distinguish the undertaking from the somewhat larger London & North Western Railway, formed just three weeks later. The scheme involved a main line from Skipton to Low Gill on the Lancaster & Carlisle, together with a branch from Clapham to Lancaster and Morecambe. The first section to open was from Lancaster to Morecambe on Whit Monday 1848. Work was proceeding on the rest of the project when the Company found it could not raise enough capital. They sought advice from Robert Stephenson who recommended that work be suspended on the Low Gill line and priority given to the easier Lancaster route.

Work south of Ingleton was so far advanced that they decided to finish it, opening from Skipton on 30 July 1849. When the route between Clapham and Lancaster was completed on 1 June 1850, they closed

A "crab" 2 – 6 – 0 entering the north end of Stainforth Tunnel (120 yards) in the 1930s.
(D Ibbotson)

Ruston & Hornsby 0 – 4 – 0 diesels "Rayleigh" and "Ramsay" inside their shed at Horton in Ribblesdale Quarry on 16 August 1965. *(John Holroyd)*

Clapham to Ingleton pending eventual extension to Low Gill.

At its opening, the "Little" North Western was single line but by summer 1853, a second track was in operation between Skipton and Hornby. The company operated its own trains until 1 June 1852, when the Midland took over the working.

Meanwhile, there was a lack of progress north of Ingleton. In 1856, the "Little" North Western tried to force the issue with a Bill to complete the line and secure running powers to both Leeds and Carlisle. The Bill was defeated on the combined opposition of the Midland, London & North Western and Lancaster & Carlisle Railways. Rejection was because of the proposed running powers, not the principle of completing the Ingleton to Low Gill line.

Though rejected, the "Little" North Western Bill of 1856 helped bring about a realignment of railway politics. It exposed the Euston Square Confederacy, a hitherto secret cartel being operated by four companies, including the LNWR and Midland, aimed largely at strangling the Great Northern Railway.

At this stage, the Midland was only a provincial railway, dependent on the LNWR for access to London. In 1857, it opened its Bedford to Hitchin extension. This brought it nearer London, to which access was now by the Great Northern. It suited the Midland to dissociate from the illegal cartel. It marked a stage in the development of the Midland towards an Anglo Scottish main line.

The "Little" North Western reintroduced its Bill in 1857. Again it was defeated but for a totally different reason. Instead of wasting money opposing the Ingleton to Low Gill link, the Lancaster & Carlisle Railway decided to bid for powers to build the line themselves. Parliament preferred the L&C Bill, in which provision was made for the purchase of land and part finished works from the "Little" North Western.

At first, the Midland appeared content with this outcome, believing that the L&C was the better able of the two contenders actually to carry out the work.

In 1859, the Midland took a 999 year lease over the "Little" North Western, absorbing it completely in 1871.

Ingleton becomes the Frontier

The Midland lease over the "Little" North Western did wonders for the share price of the Lancaster & Carlisle Railway. Suddenly, there were two potential suitors. The LNWR secured the L&C and Ingleton became a frontier even before it was built.

In 1858, the Lancaster & Carlisle deposited a Bill to vary the junction at Low Gill, involving a tighter curve off the Ingleton line. The "Little" North Western objected that this would slow down through traffic. The proposed radius was eased at the cost of building the eleven arch Low Gill Viaduct.

During the winter of 1860-61, the nine arch Ingleton Viaduct collapsed. The structure over the River Greta had been part complete when work was suspended in 1849. It was rebuilt in time for the line to open for goods on 24 August 1861. A passenger service began from Ingleton to Low Gill on 16 September. The Midland reopened its line from Clapham to Ingleton on 1 October 1861.

At first there were no through passenger trains, nor even connections. The LNWR built a station at the north end of Ingleton Viaduct and ran its two trains a day, Sundays excepted, from there to Tebay.

Things began to change the following year when LNWR trains were extended to the Midland Station at Ingleton. By 1866, there were four trains each way between Low Gill and Ingleton including one express. The 2.20pm from Tebay connected out of a Glasgow and Edinburgh to Euston train. With a quick change at Clapham, the Carlisle to Leeds journey was completed in a creditable 3½ hours.

The Midland gets impatient

On 1 October 1868, the Midland opened its London Extension from Bedford to St Pancras. No longer was access to London dependent on other companies.

The Midland was clearly intent on developing an

It was the difficulty of crossing this modest frontier which prompted the Midland to build the Settle & Carlisle Line. Ingleton Viaduct looking east in June 1964.

(Peter E Baughan)

A down freight passing Horton in Ribblesdale behind 47439 on 21 July 1976. The 1896 signal box closed in 1984 and burnt down in 1991.
(Tom Heavyside)

8F 2 – 8 – 0 No 48464 passing Horton in Ribblesdale with an up freight in November 1958.
(Peter Sunderland)

72009 "Clan Stewart" approaching Horton in Ribblesdale with the afternoon Carlisle to Bradford slow in July 1963.
(Peter Sunderland)

Anglo Scottish main line. Only in the short term could the LNWR frustrate it by operating Low Gil to Ingleton as a country branch line. If it were to push the Midland into building an independent route, then not only would it have failed to head off the competition but would be left with the expensive Lancaster & Carlisle lease. But if the Midland could be accommodated in a joint lease, this burden would be shared.

Negotiations to this end continued during 1864. The Lancaster & Carlisle exploited the opportunity to raise its guaranteed dividend to 10%. This the LNWR and Midland agreed but they couldn't find common ground on fares and freight charges. The LNWR insisted that charges for Midland traffic at Lancaster & Carlisle stations should be agreed jointly with recourse to arbitration. The Midland might have accepted this as a legitimate protection of LNWR local traffic. Except that Carlisle was to be counted as a Lancaster & Carlisle station. On this negotiations foundered.

The North of England Union Railway
An indication of how the Midland might project an independent route northwards came from a Bill, which appeared before Parliament in 1865. The North of England Union Railway was to leave the "Little" North Western near Settle and pass through Garsdale and Hawes, eventually reaching the North Eastern at Leyburn. From there it would strike off towards Darlington. In the ordinary course of events the scheme would have evaporated. Even if approved, the enterprise would not have attracted enough capital from such a thinly populated area.

This time things were different. The Midland took over the promotion and compensated the original sponsors for their trouble and expense. Beyond Hawes, the proposed line strayed into North Eastern territory, which the Midland respected. The Bill was terminated at Hawes, leaving the North Eastern free to approach from the other direction.

The Bill passed the Commons but never went before the House of Lords. It was withdrawn by the Midland who had the route re-surveyed on a better alignment designed for higher speeds. The ruling gradient was reduced from 1 in 70 to 1 in 100. The Bill was resubmitted in 1866 but it wasn't just from Settle to Hawes. It was from Settle to Carlisle with a branch to Hawes.

The Settle & Carlisle Line authorised
In presenting its Bill, the Midland had to persuade Parliament that it was in the public interest for it to be permitted to acquire land, build and operate an independent route to Carlisle. The case was put to Committees of both Houses by Mr Venables QC, who called witnesses. First was the Chairman of the short lived North of England Union Railway, whose Bill had passed the Commons the previous year. He naturally wished to explain how his excellent local scheme was to be carried forward by the Midland.

Strong support came from two Scottish Companies, the Glasgow & South Western and the North British. They operated into Carlisle from Glasgow and Edinburgh respectively. They claimed discrimination against their traffic by the LNWR which was firmly allied to the Caledonian Railway.

Another supporter was the Lancashre & Yorkshire Railway. This had an agreement with the LNWR, valid until 1876, to send Scottish traffic via Preston. But it had longer term ambitions to extend its Blackburn to Chatburn line to meet the Midland at Hellifield and make that its principle outlet to Scotland.

Witnesses were called from the business community in Carlisle to testify about the difficulties of despatching goods to places not on the LNWR, with resultant threat to employment in the City.

The North Eastern Railway was generally supportive but objected to the proposed entry into Carlisle. This involved crossing the Newcastle line on the level at Petteril Bridge and then running parallel to Carlisle

Ribblehead looking north in September 1964. The 1898 signal box closed in August 1969. *(Peter E Baughan)*

4 – 6 – 0 No 45112 passing Ribblehead with a down freight on 23 May 1961.
(Martin Bairstow collection)

Station Master Sharpe demonstrating the meteorological equipment in the goods yard at Ribblehead in September 1964.
(Peter E Baughan)

station. The NER preferred and obtained a junction at Petteril Bridge with Midlland running powers for the last mile and a half.

This amendment should in theory have pacified the London & North Western Railway whose initial sole objection concerned Carlisle Station which, it claimed, was too congested to accept independent Midland tracks. But the LNWR continued to oppose the Bill on principle and drew a lot of criticism for its conduct of the Ingleton branch. The LNWR tried to counter with evidence that delays to Midland traffic happened whilst on the Midland itself and not to the north of Ingleton.

Parliament was in no mood to protect the monopoly of the London & North Western Railway. The Midland Railway (Settle & Carlisle) Bill became an Act on 16 July 1866.

Failed Amalgamation

Just a month later, the Midland became alarmed at the prospect of an amalgamation in which its Scottish ally, the Glasgow & South Western, would be swallowed up by the Caledonian Railway. The latter company operated the most direct line from Carlisle to Glasgow via Beattock in close association with the LNWR. The GSWR offered a longer route from Gretna Junction, just on the Border, via Dumfries and Kilmarnock. It had running powers over the Caledonian for the eight miles from Carlisle to Gretna Junction.

The Midland made its own amalgamation offer to the GSWR on terms which outbid the Caledonian. In 1867 a Bill was lodged in Parliament to confirm the merger, which would have created the Midland & Scottish Railway. Not all Midland shareholders were in favour. Already fearing that the Settle & Carlisle venture would affect dividends, they didn't want to support a Scottish company as well. They need not have worried.

The Amalgamation Bill passed the House of Commons but failed in the Lords, not least because it was thought premature. Until the Settle & Carlisle line was built, the two parts of the conglomerate would be physically separate. The idea was revived later but Parliament adopted a policy opposed to further amalgamations between major railway companies. This lasted until the 1923 Grouping.

Despite the failed Amalgamation, Midland traffic was routed via the Glasgow & South Western for 100 years.

Second thoughts

A feature of the nineteenth century economy was the trade cycle which recurred about every ten years and consisted of alternate periods of expansion and recession. The mid 1860s were "boom" years as witness the large number of railway schemes authorised. By the end of the decade, companies were finding difficulty raising finance and were returning to Parliament seeking powers of abandonment. The NER Melmerby to Hawes line was a case in point. – authorised in 1865 and abandoned in 1869, though revived later in a cheaper form.

The effect of the recession on the Settle & Carlisle project was to cause the Midland and LNW Railways to start speaking again. During negotiations, the Midland denied that talks were taking place and pressed on with land purchase and other preliminaries for the new line.

On 1 February 1868, somebody sent a forged letter to the Stock Exchange purporting to come from the Midland announcing that the Settle & Carlisle scheme was to be abandoned following agreement with the LNWR. The object was doubtless to push up the share price. The Midland issued a denial and offered £50 reward (a huge sum) for information leading to detection of the culprit.

But the forged letter was close to the truth. Just four days earlier, the Chairman of the LNWR had written to the Midland proposing running powers or a joint lease between Ingleton and Carlisle. Discussions lasted several months but agreement

42492 approaching Ribblehead Viaduct with the afternoon Hellifield – Hawes on 10 January 1959. *(J C W Halliday)*

was reached in November 1868 for joint use of the line with none of the conditions, which had caused negotiations to founder three years earlier.

A Bill came before Parliament in April 1869 to abandon the Settle & Carlisle project and confirm the joint lease over the Lancaster & Carlisle. Again the Midland was represented by Mr Venables QC. This time he worked alongside Counsel for the LNWR but was opposed by the very same parties who had supported him on the original Bill.

The promoters of the erstwhile North of England Union Railway claimed that they were being cheated. Their line had been approved then taken over by the Midland who now proposed to abandon it. The Midland response was that their independent scheme would have failed anyway for want of finance.

The GSWR and North British claimed that they needed the Midland at Carlisle to avoid dependence on the monopoly of the LNWR. Mr Venables QC assured them that the Midland would be coming to Carlisle as joint lessee of the line from Ingleton. The North British said that they would still lose traffic to intermediate points on the Settle & Carlisle. Mr Venables QC agreed that abandonment would present a problem for potential traffic between Aberdeen and Hawes – if there were any.

Counsel for the Lancashire & Yorkshire said that his client enjoyed friendly relations with the LNWR to whom Scottish traffic was handed over at Preston, but they had to cover for the day when they might fall out with the LNWR. Mr Venables said that the more he read the L&Y evidence, the less he could understand why they had any objection at all to the Bill.

Basically, the Companies petitioning against the Abandonment Bill objected to having been used by the Midland to force the LNWR into negotiation. The case for abandonment was overwhelming. But the decision lay with a Committee of MPs who didn't like being used either. They expressed their feeling by rejecting the Bill. The Midland was committed to build the Settle & Carlisle

Of course, if the Midland had simply failed to build the line, the scheme would have gone the way, which the Midland itself had predicted for the North of England Union. But the Midland would have been left terminating at Ingleton. The joint lease had been rejected, leaving the Lancaster & Carlisle still on 8%. Preliminary work on the Settle & Carlisle resumed straight away, ready for actual construction to begin in November 1869.

Work gets underway
The 71 mile route was divided into four contracts. No 1 covered 17 miles from Settle Junction to Dent Head. This was possibly the most difficult stretch. It proved to be the most troublesome. It was let to John Ashwell of Kentish Town in September 1869.

Contract No 2, again about 17 miles extending to Smardale, was let in November to Benton &

A 4F 0 – 6 – 0 crossing Ribblehead Viaduct with a northbound freight in 1946.
(W Hubert Foster, courtesy John Holroyd)

LMS 8F 2 – 8 – 0 No 8177 draws up to the water column in the up goods loop at Blea Moor in 1946.
(W Hubert Foster, courtesy John Holroyd)

A 4F 0 – 6 – 0 approaching Blea Moor Tunnel with a north bound freight in July 1960. *(Peter Sunderland)*

"Black Five" 4 – 6 – 0 No 44900 has just passed Ribblehead with a down freight in 1958.
(Martin Bairstow collection)

A class WD 2 – 8 – 0 heading an engineer's train over Arten Gill Viaduct on 22 August 1964.
(Peter E Baughan)

Woodiwiss. No 3 covered 14 ½ miles as far as New Biggin and was awarded to Joseph Firbank in March 1870. The fourth contract went to Eckersley & Bayliss in April 1870, taking the line to Petteril Bridge Junction.

Up to 7,000 men were employed. Some were local but many were migrants who had worked on railway projects elsewhere. They lived in shanty towns, bringing their families to live in wooden huts with black felt roofs in settlements which acquired names including Inkerman, Sebastapol, Salt Lake City, Jericho and Belgravia.

Wages were comparatively high but some of the men on piece rate used to stop work by mid afternoon when they had earned enough, much to the annoyance of the contractors and Railway Company. In the more pastoral areas at the northern end, labour used to drift away at haymaking time.

The shanty towns were provided with Sunday schools, shops and drinking houses. The Railway paid the salary of a preacher to look after the spiritual needs of the men on contract No 1, allowing him a free pass between Bradford and Settle once a month. Another scripture reader was based at Kirkby Stephen, part of the Company's effort to protect the resident population here and at Appleby from the threat of disorder.

No work took place on a Sunday, meaning that Saturday evenings could get a bit lively. Drink was a problem. The Ingleton Constabulary was kept busy policing the area around Ribblehead, described by their Inspector as a very lawless place, where tradesmen were afraid to go. Leisure pursuits amongst the navvies included bare fist and cock fighting.

An ex navvy called Pollen had risen in the world to run a shop and had also become the local undertaker. By 1873, he claimed to have delivered 110 bodies to the small churchyard at Chapel Le Dale, a statistic apparently confirmed by the vicar. The churchyard had to be extended. The Midland Railway also paid for an extension to the burial ground at Cowgill in consequence of the number of fatalities at Blea Moor.

Deaths arose though all manner of causes. There were accidents at work, some possibly brought on by drink. Some navvies were killed in fights. Many deaths were from natural causes, especially among infants. There was an outbreak of smallpox at Ribblehead in 1871. Fortunately this was contained. The contractor provided a hospital in which to isolate the sufferers.

As work progressed it was found that the surveyors had under estimated certain problems. It had not been intended to build a viaduct at Dandry Mire, just north of Garsdale. But the mire just swallowed up the material which was tipped over three years in the attempt to make an embankment. The length of Blea Moor Tunnel as planned was only 2,112 yards but it had to be extended southwards by 308 yards and by 66 yards at the north end because of the difficulty of making cuttings and to avoid an aqueduct.

Miles of temporary track were laid to bring materials to site from the nearest access points. Forty years into the Railway Age, the Settle & Carlisle

Garsdale, or Dandrymire, Viaduct looking north.   *(W Hubert Foster, courtesy John Holroyd)*

"Black Five" No 44903 with an up passenger train south of Dent on 22 August 1964. *(Peter E Baughan)*

Dent station snowed up during January 1947, when the Settle & Carlisle line was blocked as a through route for two months. *(W Hubert Foster, courtesy John Holroyd)*

Troops clearing the snow in 1947.   *(W Hubert Foster, courtesy John Holroyd)*

Stanier "Black Five" No 44993 passing Dent with a down relief train in July 1960.   *(Peter Sunderland)*

navvies had much more by way of mechanical aid than had the pioneers. Wooden scaffolding was erected around the viaducts. This formed a crude track upon which steam operate "travellers" could operate like an overhead travelling crane.

Dynamite was used instead of gunpowder to blast through rock. It had to be brought the whole way from Carlisle or Newcastle by road. It was not allowed to be carried by train as it didn't live too comfortably with a steam locomotive.

Ashwell had evidently tendered too low a price for the No 1 contract and was in difficulty from the start. He was required to complete the first 12 miles to Ribbehead by the end of June 1871 and to have the whole of his contract ready for opening on 1 May 1873. All four contracts were behind, but Ashwell was the first to ask the Railway to lend him money. At first the Company complied but later decided that Ashwell lacked the resources to complete this most difficult stretch, which included Ribblehead Viaduct and Blea Moor Tunnel. The contract was cancelled in October 1871, the Railway taking on direct responsibility for the work.

Messrs Eckersley and Bayliss on contract No 4 managed to part company but Bayliss continued with the aid of a loan from the Midland, secured on his plant. In a bid to recruit more men, Bayliss provided huts with boarded floors and bedding. He also operated a sick fund.

Work was not helped by the weather. 1872 saw rainfall about 50% more than average for the district. By the start of 1873, a temporary track was in place between Settle Junction and Ribblehead. This made it a great deal easier to get materials to the incomplete works further north.

It had been hoped to have the whole line in operation by 1873 but this was totally unrealistic. The only part which was opened that year was the first 3½ miles from Settle Junction to the quarry at Stainforth.

It took until 2 August 1875 for the first goods trains to run right through to Carlisle. At first there was only one track between Hawes Junction and Mallerstang but the second line was in use from 4 October.

In business at last

The Settle & Carlisle line opened to passenger traffic on May Day 1876. In view of all the difficulties, it was an incredible achievement in just seven years from rejection of the Abandonment Bill.

On the opening day, the first through Pullman Cars left St Pancras at 10.30 in the morning. Orders for lunch were collected at Leicester and telegraphed to Normanton so that no part of the 30 minute refreshment (and toilet) stop would be wasted.

The train reversed direction at Leeds, where a fresh engine was attached for the journey through the Aire Valley to the new station at Skipton. Here the Edinburgh and Glasgow portions were split, both continuing non-stop to Carlisle, 12 minutes apart, in exactly two hours. The Edinburgh train then travelled over the Waverley route to reach the Scottish capital at 9.15pm. Five minutes later, the Glasgow train was steaming into that City's St Enoch terminus.

North Eastern Connections

The North Eastern Railway had been generally supportive of the Settle & Carlisle project. Once they'd agreed arrangements at Petteril Bridge and Hawes, there was nothing which could pose any threat to the North Eastern. The two railways came alongside one another at Appleby, where a connection was made but not developed as originally hoped.

The line from Kirkby Stephen (East) to Clifton near Penrith had been promoted as the Eden Valley Railway. When it opened in 1862, it was first worked then taken over by the Stockton & Darlington Railway, which was itself absorbed by the North Eastern a year later.

St Leonard's Church, Chapel–Le-Dale, where the vicar had to solicit a contribution from the Midland Railway towards extension of the burial ground.
(Peter E Baughan)

Class 9F No 92012 passing Dent with an up freight on 22 August 1964. *(Peter E Baughan)*

Garsdale water troughs were commissioned in 1907 on a level stretch between Rise Hill Tunnel and Garsdale Station. *(W H Foster, courtesy John Holroyd)*

"Black Five" 4 – 6 – 0 No 44933 passing Garsdale with the Saturday Heads of Ayr to Leeds in July 1963. A 4F hauled freight has set back into the bay platform to be overtaken. *(Peter Sunderland)*

8F 2 – 8 – 0 No 48426 passing Garsdale with a southbound freight in July 1963. *(Peter Sunderland)*

The single platform Appleby Station opened on 9 June 1862. It was designated Appleby East in 1952, when the almost adjacent Midland Station became Appleby West. It closed on 20 January 1962 and is now a scrap yard.

For most of its 100 years, Appleby East saw three trains each way between Darlington and Penrith. The main traffic on the Stainmore Line was iron ore between Cumbria and the blast furnaces on Teesside.

Immediately north of the two Appleby stations, the Midland built a double track connection just over ¼ mile in length. It was more than would have been required just for the exchange of goods traffic. The Midland had its eye on Penrith and the northern Lakes and asked the North Eastern to augment its service with trains specially timed to connect with Midland expresses. From July 1880, the Midland paid the North Eastern to run three trains each way non stop from Appleby (Midland) to Penrith. They lasted 13 years, presumably on a seasonal basis. After that, the proximity of the Lake District to the Settle & Carlisle line was never exploited. From 1 July 1910, the Midland attacked Penrith a different way by diverting one St Pancras to Scotland express to run non stop from Leeds to Penrith via Ingleton. A seasonal service was offered up to the First World War using informal running powers over the LNWR, with whom relations were on a more mature footing.

The original idea of the Midland was for a more substantial integration with the North Eastern at Appleby. Under the Midland Act of June 1875, a second connection was authorised south of the two stations, cutting through the later Express Dairy siding. This would have given access from Darlington onto the Midland and it may have been intended to route passenger traffic through the Midland Station and close Appleby East.

The Midland work on the South Junction link was completed in 1877 but the North Eastern never laid the junction at their end.

Blackburn to Hellifield

The final stage of the Settle & Carlisle project was achieved in 1880, when the Lancashire & Yorkshire Railway completed its extension from Chatburn to Hellifield. Here an enlarged station was provided by the Midland, half a mile west of the previous "Little" North Western structure.

The railway had reached Chatburn in 1850 but a proposal to extend to Elslack on the Colne to Skipton line was abandoned for lack of finance. So was an 1864 scheme to reach Long Preston. Only when the Settle & Carlisle was actually under construction, did the L&Y make serious efforts to project itself north from Chatburn. The line to Hellifield was authorised in 1871 but proceeded slowly. When it was ready for use in 1879, the Board of Trade Inspector refused permission to open beyond Gisburn because the Midland was lagging behind with the new Hellifield station.

Comprising a large island platform with extensive canopies and a bay at each end, the station was brought into use on 1 June 1880, along with the line from Gisburn. This opened a new route from Manchester and Liverpool to Scotland. Hellifield was provided with an engine shed and extensive exchange sidings.

To accommodate Midland Pullman coaches, restricted clearances had to be eased on the route from Manchester. The L&Y built a second tunnel at Farnworth (near Bolton), so as to run one track through each, and lowered the track through Sough Tunnel (south of Darwen). The Manchester to Hellifield route is featured in *Railways in East Lancashire*.

Midland compound 4 – 4 – 0 No 1018 crossing Lunds Viaduct with an up express in 1946.
(W Hubert Foster, courtesy John Holroyd)

The stockaded turntable at Garsdale. *(W Hubert Foster, courtesy John Holroyd)*

Stanier 8F 2 – 8 – 0 No 8126 approaching Ais Gill with an up freight in 1950.
(W Hubert Foster, courtesy John Holroyd)

The 1890 signal box at Ais Gill was closed in 1981 but recommissioned at Butterley on the preserved Midland Railway three years later. *(Peter E Baughan)*

2 – 8 – 0 No 48505 passing Ais Gill on 14 September 1967 with three condemned diesel locos. Andrew Barclay D2441 would have been class 06. North British Loco Co hydraulics D2712 and D2752 had lasted less than ten years. The doomed steam loco had managed 23 years. *(Martin Bairstow collection)*

A class 47 approaching Birkett Tunnel, north of Mallerstang with the 8.25 Leeds to Carlisle on 22 August 1989.
(David A Smith)

The Midland Railway endowed Kirkby Stephen with one of the larger style "Derby Gothic" buildings. Unfortunately, it was 1½ miles from the town.
(John Sagar)

Passenger Services

For the first 94 years, from its opening in 1876, the Settle & Carlisle Line offered quite distinct express and local services. Details are shown for three representative years: 1880 when the route was fairly new, 1910 when it was close to its zenith and 1960 when it was in decline but still operating to traditional principles. Finally, the radically different 1993 timetable is featured.

The Midland express trains offered at least as good a standard of comfort as was available on competing lines. In this way the company tried to compensate for its slightly more difficult route.

Fastest Journey times in 1910

	London to Glasgow			London to Edinburgh		
	Miles	Hours	Mins	Miles	Hours	Mins
West Coast	401½	8	15	400	8	15
East Coast	440¼	9	35	393	8	15
Midland	424	9	5	406¾	8	40

The East Coast route was not really able to compete on London–Glasgow journey times. The situation is different today. Glasgow can be reached in 5 hours from Euston or 5¼ from Kings Cross but Edinburgh is only 4¼ hours away from Kings Cross. Nowadays the Midland route does not enter the comparison.

The local service was slow taking around 2¼ hours for the 76¾ miles between Hellifield and Carlisle with 20 intermediate stops.

In *Rails in the Fells,* David Jenkinson considers the part played by the railway in the progress of the local communities. The railway companies employed plenty of staff to collate statistics and records exist of the number of tickets issued at every station. The practice continued well into BR days though some data for the LMS period was lost.

Of the 20 stations on the Settle & Carlisle line (including Hawes), the busiest was Settle with some 30,000 bookings per annum in the pre-grouping period. Appleby managed about 20,000. Horton-in-Ribblesdale, Hawes Junction, Lazonby, Armathwaite, Cumwhinton and Scotby achieved around 10,000. All the others were a good deal less with Ribblehead and Dent managing only around 3,000, the equivalent of ten per day for a six day week. There may have been incoming passengers as well plus season tickets.

Dent, apparently issued one season ticket in the 46 years between 1876 and 1922, presumably for a period of one year. Ribblehead did better with 13. There appears to have been a commuter there for 4 years around 1900 then another one for the last 9 years of Midland ownership.

Season ticket issues were more worthwhile at stations closer to Carlisle with an average of ten a year being issued at Lazonby and Cumwhinton. Commuters were most in evidence at Settle where an average of 60 season tickets were issued each year during the Midland period. Some of these would have been for quite long distances such as to Bradford or Leeds.

By 1960, the number of local travellers had fallen with only Settle and Appleby station selling 10,000 tickets

An express prepares to leave Carlisle for Leeds on what is now platform 3, about 1905. An immaculate 2 – 4 – 0 leads a 4 – 4 – 0. *(Peter E Baughan collection)*

The detached Station Master's House at Kirby Stephen with six terraced cottages for the lower grades.
(Martin Bairstow)

The North Eastern Station at Kirkby Stephen was more convenient to the town but it closed in 1962. "Standard" 2 – 6 – 0 No 76045 pilots Ivatt 2 – 6 – 0 No 43126 with a Saturdays only Blackpool – Newcastle on 25 June 1960.
(Peter Hutchinson)

Crosby Garrett looking south in Midland days.
(Peter E Baughan collection)

a year. Six of the 20 stations had closed. Some of those still open were issuing less than 1,000 tickets per year – an average of only two per day.

Because the LMS figures are missing, it is not known exactly when the rot set in. The advent of motor transport had·removed people's dependence on the railway which had done nothing to exploit new traffic opportunities.

What remained of the local traffic was discarded in 1970 but the express trains still catered for a worthwhile volume of through traffic until 1982 when much of this was diverted away.

Today there are still some longer distance travellers and there are commuters both from Settle towards Leeds and from Eden Valley stations into Carlisle. The line is popular with ramblers including some individuals who travel almost every week. During the period of threatened closure, a lot of people were drawn to the line by newspaper and media publicity. Whilst some of this novelty may have waned, there are still plenty of passengers travelling just for a day out over a scenic route. Also arising from the publicity of the closure period, are the coach tours which include a trip over the line often for a single journey between Settle and Carlisle or between Settle and Appleby.

There are many small traffic flows such as shopping trips and visits to friends and relations. Taken together, these various classes of traffic add up to more passengers in total than were ever seen in the past, especially at some of the intermediate stations.

SETTLE & CARLISLE LINE

Northbound Passenger Service 1880

Depart
Hellifield

—	Pullman sleeping cars to Glasgow and Edinburgh (9.15 pm from St. Pancras, 1.50 am from Leeds)
7.17 am	Local to Carlisle
11.35 am	Express to Glasgow and Edinburgh (10.00 am from Manchester and 10.32 am from Leeds)
11.50 am	Local to Carlisle
4.06 pm	Express to Edinburgh (3.00 pm from Leeds)
—	Pullman Parlour Car to Glasgow (10.35 am ex St. Pancras, 4.05 pm ex Leeds)
4.47 pm	Local to Carlisle

No trains at all on Sundays apart from the overnight service which ran every day.

Expresses generally stopped only at Appleby whilst locals stopped at every station. The 11.35 am, which included through carriages from Manchester over the newly completed Chatburn to Hellifield line, at Settle then had some complicated request stops:

Hawes Junction Kirkby Stephen	When required to take up for Carlisle and beyond.
Lazonby	To set down on cattle sale days on informing the guard at Appleby.
Armathwaite	When required to set down from L&Y stations.

At this time there were three trains per day, non stop from the Midland Station at Appleby to Penrith. They were timed to connect with expresses from the South.

There were three trains daily from Hawes Junction to Hawes, all worked by the NER at 10.45 am, 1.05 pm and 6.20 pm, the last two connecting with Locals from Hellifield.

1910

Depart
Hellifield

—	Sleeping Car Express to Glasgow and Stranraer (8.15 pm from St. Pancras, 12.38 am from Leeds)
2.42 am	Sleeping Car Express to Edinburgh (9.30 pm from St. Pancras, 1.50 am from Leeds) (also through carriages from Manchester and Liverpool)
2.52 am	Sleeping Car Express to Glasgow (9.30 pm from St. Pancras, 2.00 am from Leeds) (also through carriages from Manchester and Liverpool)
—	Sleeping Car Express to Glasgow (12.00 from St. Pancras, 4.08 am from Leeds)
7.30 am	Local to Settle
8.00 am	Local to Carlisle
10.00 am	Local to Carlisle
11.04 am	Express to Edinburgh and Glasgow (9.25 from Liverpool, 9.32 from Manchester)
11.41 am	Local to Carlisle
2.24 pm	Express to Edinburgh and Glasgow (9.30 am from St. Pancras, 1.33 pm from Leeds)
2.29 pm	Local to Hawes Junction
4.24 pm	Express to Glasgow (11.30 am from St. Pancras, 3.32 am from Leeds)
4.32 pm	Express to Edinburgh (stops at Appleby) (11.30 am from St. Pancras, 3.32 am from Leeds)
5.05 pm	Local to Carlisle
6.27 pm	Express to Glasgow (1.30 pm from St. Pancras, 5.37 pm from Leeds)
6.38 pm	Local to Horton-in-Ribblesdale
9.52 pm	SO Local to Horton-in-Ribblesdale

No trains at all on Sundays apart from the four overnight services which ran every day.

1960

3.23 am	Express to Edinburgh (stops at Appleby) (9.10 pm from St. Pancras, 2.19 am from Leeds)
—	Express to Glasgow (9.25 pm from St. Pancras, 3.04 am from Leeds)
6.05 am	Local to Garsdale
11.39 am	Express to Glasgow (stops at Appleby) (10.35 am from Leeds)
11.57 am	Local to Carlisle
2.45 pm	Express 'The Waverley' to Edinburgh (stops at Appleby) (9.10 am from St. Pancras, 1.49 pm from Leeds)
—	Thames Clyde Express to Glasgow (10.10 am from St. Pancras, 2.46 pm from Leeds
5.05 pm	Local to Carlisle

No trains at all on Sundays apart from the two overnight services which ran every day.

The 2.10 pm local to Garsdale and Hawes had ceased the previous year.

1993

Few trains now stop at Hellifield whilst all are now through from Leeds.

Depart Leeds	Depart Settle	
6.01 am SX	6.55 am SX	Local to Carlisle
6.35 am SO	7.32 am SO	,,
8.45 am	9.47 am	,,
9.49 am	10.53 am	,,
10.49 am	11.46 am	,,
12.49 am	1.45 pm	,,
2.49 pm SX	3.45 pm SX	,,
3.17 pm SO	4.17 pm SO	,,
5.25 pm	6.39 pm	,,
6.33 pm	7.45 pm	Horton and Ribblehead
SUNDAYS		
9.00 am	9.58 am	Local to Carlisle
1.32 pm	2.27 pm	,,
5.32 pm	6.33 pm	,,

The 9.49 am from Leeds and the 3 Sunday trains run only in Summer.

B. 7312 R

LMS

RACING and SPORTS at APPLEBY

Whit Monday, 21st May, 1934

Cook's DAY EXCURSION

TO

APPLEBY

FROM	Leaving at	Third Class Return Fares
	a.m.	s. d.
CARLISLE (Citadel)	11 15	3 6
SCOTBY	11 20	3 0
CUMWHINTON	11 25	3 0
COTEHILL	11 32	2 6
ARMATHWAITE	11 40	2 6
LAZONBY	11 50	1 6
LITTLE SALKELD	11 55	1 6
LANGWATHBY	12 1	1 6
CULGAITH	12 8	1 0
NEWBIGGIN	12 12	0 10
LONG MARTON	12 20	0 5

Arriving APPLEBY at 12.30 p.m.

RETURN ARRANGEMENTS.
Passengers return from APPLEBY at 6.35 p.m. same day.

Passengers are requested to obtain their Tickets in advance, as this will assist the Company in the provision of accommodation.

Have you obtained your copy of L M S INEXPENSIVE HOLIDAYS LAND CRUISE PAMPHLET ? If not, apply at any L M S Station or Enquiry Office.

Children under three years of age, Free ; three and under fourteen, half-fare.

CONDITIONS OF ISSUE OF EXCURSION TICKETS AND OTHER TICKETS AT LESS THAN ORDINARY FARE.—These Tickets are issued subject to the Notices and Conditions shown in the Company's current Time Tables. For Luggage Allowances also see Time Tables.

All information regarding Excursions and Cheap Fares and all Railway Travel and Transport can be obtained at LMS Stations, or from Mr. W. BELL, District Goods and Passenger Manager, Carlisle.

May, 1934.   A. DAVIES, Chief Commercial Manager.
E.R.O. 53302.

WA—1/5/34—No. 1—2/N.   John Horn, Ltd., Glasgow and London

B. 7313

LMS

WHIT MONDAY

21st MAY, 1934

Cook's CHEAP TICKETS to
SCOTBY, CUMWHINTON, COTEHILL,
ARMATHWAITE, LAZONBY,
LITTLE SALKELD, LANGWATHBY,
KIRKBY STEPHEN and HAWES JUNCTION

See separate announcement for Bookings to APPLEBY

FROM	LEAVING AT			RETURN ARRANGEMENTS.
	To all Stations.	To Scotby, Cumwhinton, Cotehill, Armathwaite and Lazonby.	To Scotby, Cumwhinton, Cotehill, Armathwaite, Lazonby, Little Salkeld and Langwathby only.	Passengers return by any Ordinary Train same day.
	a.m. a.m.	p.m.	p.m.	
CARLISLE	8 3 10 40	1 45	4 22	
SCOTBY	8 10 10 47	1 50	4 29	Additional Service
CUMWHINTON	8 14 10 50	1 55	4 33	
COTEHILL	8 20 10 57	2 2	4 39	p.m.
ARMATHWAITE	8 27 11 4	2 9	4 46	Lazonby ......lve. 5 0
LAZONBY	8 36 11 13	2 18	4 56	Armathwaite ,, 5 10
LITTLE SALKELD	8 42 11 19	—	5 2	Cotehill .... ,, 5 15
LANGWATHBY	8 46 11 23	—	—	Cumwhinton ,, 5 20
	p.m.			Scotby ...... ,, 5 29
KIRKBY STEPHEN	9 39 12 13	—	—	Carlisle ...... arr. 5 35

FOR FARES SEE OTHER SIDE

Passengers are requested to obtain their Tickets in advance, as this will assist the Company in the provision of accommodation.

Have you obtained your copy of L M S INEXPENSIVE HOLIDAYS LAND CRUISE PAMPHLET ? If not, apply at any L M S Station or Enquiry Office.

CHILDREN under three years of age, Free ; three years and under fourteen, Half-fare.

CONDITIONS OF ISSUE OF EXCURSION TICKETS AND OTHER TICKETS AT LESS THAN ORDINARY FARE.—These Tickets are issued subject to the Notices and Conditions shown in the Company's Current Time Tables. For luggage allowances also see Time Tables.

All information regarding Excursions and Cheap Fares and all Railway Travel and Transport can be obtained at L M S Stations, or from Mr. W. Bell, District Goods and Passenger Manager, Carlisle.

May, 1934.   A. DAVIES, Chief Commercial Manager
E.R.O. 53303.

WA—1/5/34—No. 2-2/N.   [Over

Crosby Garrett looking north.

(W Hubert Foster, courtesy John Holroyd)

A three car Metro Cammell unit crossing Crosby Garrett Viaduct with the 13.03 from Leeds to Carlisle on 22 August 1989. *(David A Smith)*

Midland 2P class 4 – 4 – 0 No 720 calls at Ormside with an up local about 1946.
(W Hubert Foster, courtesy John Holroyd)

Ormside Viaduct. Carlisle is to the right.

(W Hubert Foster, courtesy John Holroyd)

"Milk for London". The dairy siding just south of Appleby Station about 1946.

(W Hubert Foster, courtesy John Holroyd)

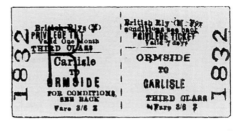

48472 passing Appleby with an up freight in July 1960.
(Peter Sunderland)

Long Marton looking north in September 1963.
(Peter E Baughan)

Local Freight Traffic

As with passengers, the bulk of freight carried over the Settle & Carlisle line was long distance. Goods facilities were however available at all 20 stations between Settle and Scotby, including Hawes.

The Midland Railway recorded freight in four categories – livestock; coal, coke, lime and limestone; other minerals and general merchandise.

In the early years from 1876, a total of some 6,000 wagon loads of sheep or cattle were dispatched from the 15 stations which handled this traffic. Ormside, Culgaith, Little Salkeld, Cotehill and Cumwhinton had no loading facilities. By the 1923 Grouping, the annual tally had reached nearly 10,000 wagons, a quarter of which originate from Lazonby with Settle, Hawes and Appleby also recording over 1,000 wagons each.

Livestock traffic proved easy prey to the advent of motorised road transport which avoided the trouble and loss of weight involved in herding the animals to the station, feeding them en route and so on. By the 1950s, BR was loading only a few hundred wagons a year from all the Settle & Carlisle stations combined. It soon dried up completely.

Traffic in the coal and lime category started at an annual rate of about 100,000 tons, half of it at Settle. By the turn of the twentieth century, quarry output at Horton in Ribblesdale had pushed the total nearer to 150,000 tons. Most of the smaller stations managed 1,000 tons annually, the equivalent of two wagons per week. By the early 1960s, the total was down to 35,000 tons a year, most of it at Horton in Ribblesdale.

The "other minerals" category showed a steady increase from 1876 right into BR days with annual tonnage increasing from 25,000 to something over 600,000 in the 1950s. The bulk of this arose at Horton in Ribblesdale, at Kirkby Thore Gypsum Siding near New Biggin and at Long Meg near Lazonby.

"General merchandise" included everything which did not fit into the other three categories. In Midland days, only Settle, New Biggin, Cotehill and Cumwhinton achieved more than 10,000 tons per year. The last three would be explained by traffic from Kirkby Thore and from brick and plaster works further north, which was classed as general merchandise when carried in less than full wagon loads. Traffic from private sidings was added to that of the nearest station for statistical purposes.

Overall in the 1950s and early 60s, British Railways were handling more than double the local freight tonnage that the Midland had ever done. This was thanks almost entirely to the quarry at Long Meg.

2 – 6 – 0 No 43130 shunting Ribblehead Quarry on 3 September 1964. *(Peter E Baughan)*

2 – 6 – 0 No 43036 shunts out of Appleby West goods yard on 22 August 1964.

(Peter E Baughan)

A goods train waits the passage of a southbound passenger before it can shunt across into the sidings at Long Meg on 24 September 1963.

(Peter E Baughan)

Shunting the plaster works at the end of Howe & Cos Siding in June 1969, 0 – 4 – 0ST "J N Derbyshire" was built by Andrew Barclay, Kilmarnock in 1929. It is preserved at the Ribble Steam Railway, Preston along with "John Howe" of 1908.   *(Mike McCormac)*

New Biggin looking north in September 1963.
(Peter E Baughan)

Culgaith did not open until 1 April 1880 and was in different style to the others. It closed on 2 May 1970.
(Peter E Baughan collection)

"Black Five" 4 – 6 – 0 No 45217 passing Langwathby with an up freight on 20 April 1965.
(Peter Hutchinson)

40090 passing the closed station at Culgaith with a freight from Carlisle to Healey Mills on 23 September 1982. *(Tom Heavyside)*

LMS compound 4 – 4 – 0 No 1075 emerging from the south end of Culgaith Tunnel (661 yards) in the 1930s. *(D Ibbotson)*

Little Salkeld looking north in May 1978, eight years after closure. It is substantially the same today. *(Alan Young)*

156 479 calls at Armathwaite on 2 July 1993. Up waiting room in use. The platform has since been raised making the steps redundant. *(John Sagar)*

The 1900 box still in use at Low House Crossing. *(John Sagar)*

"Crab" 2 – 6 – 0 No 13062 (later 42762) emerging from the north end of Armathwaite Tunnel (325 yards) in the 1930s. *(D Ibbotson)*

2 – 6 – 4T No 42313 leaving Armathwaite with the 6.05pm Carlisle to Appleby local on 5 June 1962. *(R Leslie)*

Cotehill, closed on 5 April 1952, looking north in April 1974. It has since been demolished.
(Alan Young)

144 016 passing the 1916 signal box at Howe & Cos Siding on 2 July 1993. *(John Sagar)*

Cumwhinton looking south in April 1977. It is still there despite closure on 3 November 1956. The next station, Scotby, closed on 31 January 1942. The main building there is now a private house.
(Alan Young)

Armathwaite Signal Box, restored as a non operational exhibit. *(John Sagar)*

Cumwhinton up platform looking south in September 1963. *(Peter E Baughan)*

0 – 4 – 0ST "J N Derbyshire" shunting the exchange siding at Howe & Cos on 14 June 1969.
(Mike McCormac)

60096 "Papyrus" has just arrived at Carlisle with the up "Waverley" from Edinburgh on 5 September 1959. "Black Five" 45029 and a "Jubilee" (not visible) wait on the adjacent track to take the train on to Leeds.   (M Mitchell)

Class A3 4 – 6 – 2 No 60094 "Colorado" is ready to take "The Waverley" on the next leg of its journey to Edinburgh.   (J C W Halliday)

The Hawes Branch

Midland 2P 4 – 4 – 0 at Hawes with the afternoon "Bonnyface", about 1946.
(W Hubert Foster, courtesy John Holroyd)

The market town of Hawes lies some six miles east of the Settle & Carlisle line. Powers for the single track branch were included in the 1866 Act, which subsumed the North of England Union scheme. The work was put out to tender during 1871 and the contract (No 5) awarded to Benton & Woodiwiss who also held the adjacent No 2 contract on the main line.

Low priority was given to the branch which was not completed until 1878. The line followed the valley of the River Ure, which flows through Wensleydale. The maximum gradient was 1 in 69 falling towards Hawes.

Two miles from Hawes Junction, the line pierced Mossdale Head with a 245 yard tunnel. This was followed by a four arch viaduct over the Mossdale Beck. Then a mile short of Hawes came the five arch Appersett Viaduct.

The station at Hawes Junction had opened on 1 August 1876, three months after the Settle & Carlisle line. Its main purpose was interchange, hence the

layout with the main building on the island platform. This supported a glass canopy to shelter passengers on both the up main and branch platforms. The canopy was demolished in 1957. The name of the station changed to Hawes Junction & Garsdale in 1900 and to just Garsdale in 1932.

Though owned and staffed jointly with the North Eastern, Hawes Station was distinctly Midland in appearance, in standard Settle & Carlisle style. Mile post 262¾ from St Pancras stood close to the Midland signal box at the east end of the layout. There was also a box at the west end of the station until this was replaced by a ground frame in 1907. The signals and facing point lock were then operated from the East Box but the point itself would have required a "pull" of 315 yards, hence the ground frame. The Hawes West signal box name board was fixed to a fence by the ground frame, against which it looked rather oversize.

D40 class 4 – 4 – 0 No 6238
with a Northallerton train a
Garsdale on 19 Septembe
1953.
(J W Hague, courtesy
David Beeken

Ex North Eastern Railway class
G5 0 – 4 – 4T No 67312 waits
at Hawes with a Garsdale to
Northallerton train.
(J W Hague, courtesy
David Beeken)

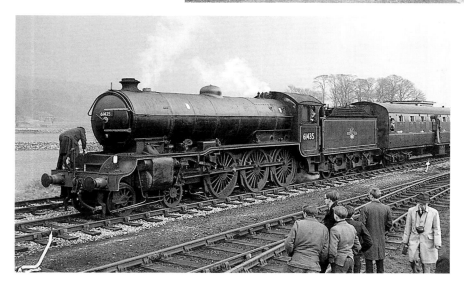

B16 class 4 – 6 – 0 No 6143!
with the last passenger train
at Hawes on 25 April 1964
The engine, built in 1922, was
scrapped later that year.
(Martin Bairstow collection,

Hawes opened in three stages at two monthly intervals during 1878. The first North Eastern goods train arrived on 1 June 1878. Then the Midland opened for goods on 1 August. Finally, the line opened for passengers right through from Leyburn to Hawes Junction on 1 October.

The service of three trains a day was provided by the North Eastern, to whom the Midland paid a fee, rather than attempt a Hawes to Hawes Junction passenger service of its own.

The Midland had built a small engine shed at Hawes Junction and may originally have been planning to operate the branch from there. In 1881, the North Eastern took a lease on the unused shed and rented some of the cottages for its staff. The train service went up to four a day with an additional evening arrival at Hawes Junction and an earlier morning departure. It remained at this level until 1939.

The usual engine stationed at Hawes Junction was a BTP (Bogie Tank Passenger) 0 – 4 – 4T. These were built from 1874 specifically to work branch passenger trains, which had previously relied on engines relegated from the main line. 124 in number, most survived until the 1920s, to become LNER class G6.

On 6 October 1917, BTP No 207 was inside Hawes Junction shed when it caught fire. The loco was badly damaged but was repaired at Darlington and ran for another three years. The shed was rebuilt. After the Grouping, the LNER kept a F8 class 2 – 4 – 2T at Hawes Junction. This gave way in 1935 to a G5 class

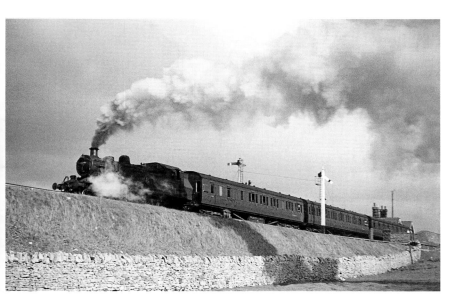

2 – 6 – 2T No 41206 has just left Ribblehead for Hawes with the usual two brake vans and composite in the middle.
(Martin Bairstow collection)

Fairburn 2 – 6 – 4T No 42484 is ready to leave Hawes with the one train of the day in June 1957. *(Peter Sunderland)*

G5 class 0 – 4 – 4T No 67314 arriving at Garsdale from Northallerton on 27 March 1954.

(N E Stead collection)

4F 0 – 6 – 0 No 43893 emerging from Mossdale Head Tunnel with the pick up goods from Hawes.

(N E Stead collection)

0 – 4 – 4T. No 435 (67346) was the regular engine until 1 May 1939 when the shed closed and Leyburn, which had been closed since 1915, reopened.

This change caused the first train out of Hawes Junction and the last return to be cancelled, taking the service back to three each way. It remained at this level until 1954, except that by the end the middle one had become Saturdays only.

About 1902, the Midland introduced an afternoon passenger train from Hellifield to Hawes and back. For reason unknown, it acquired the nickname "Bonnyface" and lasted until 1959. It was in addition to the trains operated by the North Eastern. On the outward journey only, it was allowed 10 minutes at Hawes Junction where it had to draw forward towards Carlisle, then set back over the trailing crossover into the bay platform. It was not advertised as a through train.

In 1922, there were departures from Hawes Junction at 6.55 and 10.31am, 1.05, 4.03 and 6.26pm. The 4.03 was the Midland train. The others were through to Northallerton. There was never a regular Sunday service. In the 1930s, there was an extra train on Tuesdays only at 9.16am from Garsdale, and 9.45am from Hawes. This was a market day extra worked by the North Eastern train during what was otherwise its layover in Garsdale.

About 1951, the method of single line security between Garsdale and Hawes was converted from staff and ticket to electric tablet. The sections east of Hawes had been similarly upgraded much earlier.

The Garsdale to Northallerton trains ran for the last time on 24 April 1954 but the closure didn't affect "Bonnyface". So for the next five years, Hawes saw just one passenger train a day, which arrived from Hellifield at 3.25pm and set off back an hour later. It was normally a three coach formation with two brake thirds (second from 1956) and a composite in the middle. All types of traffic were thus catered for from first class to parcels. Amongst those who actually availed of this train were railway wives on their weekly shopping free ticket. The hour in Hawes was an alternative to a longer venture to Skipton, The daily Midland goods was also still running to Hawes.

This arrangement ended on 14 March 1959 when the Garsdale to Hawes branch was closed to all traffic. It was then dismantled and the land sold off piecemeal. Hawes itself retained a goods service from the North Eastern end. The former Midland signal box closed in 1960, after which it was worked as one engine in steam from Wensley. The end came on 25 April 1964, when the line was cut back to Redmire. A special passenger train visited Hawes on the last day, organised by the Railway Correspondence and Travel Society

Today the station is part of the Dales Countryside Museum. It is well restored with track in the platforms and a three coach train headed by a loco bearing the number 67345 in honour of the last G5 to have been shedded at Leyburn. The engine is actually a 0 – 6 – 0T from Hams Hall Power Station, built in 1955. The carriages are BR mark 1s, also too young to have caught the Hawes passenger service. The detached Station Master's house offers bed and breakfast accommodation.

2 – 6 – 2T No 41206 crossing Appersett viaduct with the returning Hawes to Hellifield.

(N E Stead collection)

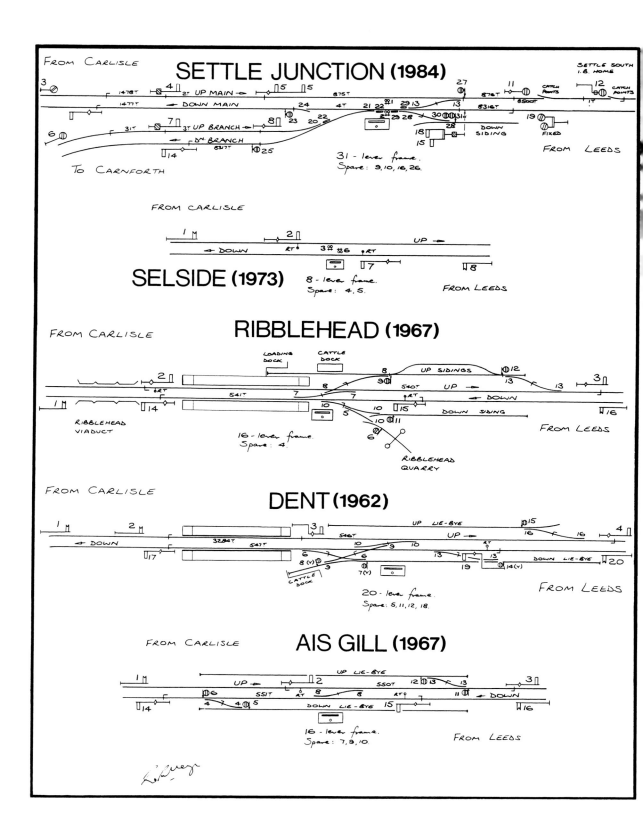

SETTLE JUNCTION (1984)

FROM CARLISLE

SETTLE SOUTH I.B. HOME

31 - lever frame.
Spare: 9, 10, 16, 26.

TO CARNFORTH

FROM LEEDS

SELSIDE (1973)

FROM CARLISLE

8 - lever frame.
Spare: 4, 5.

FROM LEEDS

RIBBLEHEAD (1967)

FROM CARLISLE

LOADING DOCK

CATTLE DOCK

UP SIDINGS

RIBBLEHEAD VIADUCT

16 - lever frame.
Spare: 4.

RIBBLEHEAD QUARRY

FROM LEEDS

DENT (1962)

FROM CARLISLE

UP LIE-BYE

CATTLE DOCK

DOWN LIE-BYE

20 - lever frame.
Spare: 5, 11, 12, 18.

FROM LEEDS

AIS GILL (1967)

FROM CARLISLE

UP LIE-BYE

DOWN LIE-BYE

16 - lever frame.
Spare: 7, 9, 10.

FROM LEEDS

Accidents

A "Royal Scot" 4 – 6 – 0 passing Kildwick & Crosshills with an up excursion in November 1963. How was the driver expected to see signals with steam leaking out like that?
(Peter Sunderland)

Although rail travel is inherently safer than most other means of transport, there have been accidents on the Leeds to Carlisle line. Below are described three of the more notorious tragedies which have taken place. These highlight the shortcomings of some early methods of operation.

Kildwick 28 August 1875

The opening of the Settle & Carlisle line coincided with the introduction of absolute block working on main lines of the Midland Railway. The route between Leeds and Settle Junction was converted from the rather unsatisfactory time interval system during 1875. Settle Junction to Carlisle was worked on the block system from the outset.

The time interval system had gone out with a bang, literally, when a mail and passenger train from Ingleton to Leeds had ploughed into the back of a returning excursion from Morecambe late in the evening of 28 August 1875.

At this stage block working was already in use between Leeds and Keighley and was about to be introduced from there to Settle Junction.

The excursion left Skipton for Leeds at 11.12 pm. As it passed Cononley, signalman Jonathan Baldwin noticed that the tail lamp was unlit so he telegraphed Kildwick 'stop and examine train'.

The Ingleton to Leeds train was in the care of driver Harrison Palfreeman. It had already been brought to a stand at Skipton North Box whilst the excursion was stopped in the station. It had then drawn forward, completed its own station business and been signalled away from Skipton five minutes behind the excursion as permitted under the time interval system. At that time the signals had three positions: 'Stop', 'Caution' and 'all right' with the respective lights of red, green

and white. Palfreeman later acknowledged that he had left Skipton under a caution signal but claimed that it was so rare to see the signal at 'all right' that he and other drivers more or less took the caution signal to mean that.

Approaching Cononley at a speed of about 40mph, Palfreeman saw the distant signal 'all right' and claimed also to have seen the home signal also showing that aspect. This latter claim was disputed by signalman Baldwin who said that it was at caution. Be that as it may, Baldwin had signalled Palfreeman's train through Cononley only 4½ minutes after the excursion had passed and in the knowledge that the excursion was going to be stopped at Kildwick home signal on his instruction. He claimed that the Kildwick distant should have been adequate protection coupled with the fact that Palfreeman's train was booked to stop at Kildwick Station and so would be slowing down.

As Palfreeman was passing Cononley, the excursion was at a stand at Kildwick. Palfreeman failed to see the Kildwick distant until he was almost on it. He crashed into the rear of the excursion train at about 15 mph. Five passengers were killed and 40 injured.

In his report to the Board of Trade, Capt Tyler censured Baldwin for not stopping the Ingleton–Leeds train at Cononley and Palfreeman for going too fast. Normally he would also have taken the Railway Company to task for repeatedly ignoring advice from himself and his colleagues of the urgency of introducing the block system. However on this occasion he acknowledged that progress was being made and that the Midland was amongst the more progressive railways in this respect.

The Kildwick accident would have been avoided under the block system. The Cononley signalman could not have given a clear signal until the previous train was within the protection of the Kildwick home signal.

Hawes Junction – 24 December 1910

There are two accidents which stand out in the history of the Settle & Carlisle Line. They happened within three years of one another and no more than three miles apart. Both revealed serious weaknesses in the operation of the Railway but what made them particularly horrific were the fires which followed the collisions.

Originally there had been two signal boxes at Hawes Junction. However from 10 July 1910, the functions of the previous North and South boxes were amalgamated into the new larger box which still stands part way along the northbound platform. This created a long 'station limit' with the need for both starter and advanced starter signals. It was in the early morning of Christmas Eve 1910 that disaster struck.

Alfred Sutton had been a signalman at Hawes Junction for at least 20 years. He had 'booked on' at 8 pm on the evening of 23 December. It was a foul night. In addition to a steady flow of passenger and goods trains in each direction, there was also a busy traffic in light engines. Many trains needed pilot engines for the uphill journey from either Carlisle or Leeds (or sometimes just from Hellifield). These usually came off at Hawes Junction so that they could return light engine.

By five in the morning, there were five engines in the sidings at Hawes Junction waiting to return home. Two of them, Nos. 448 and 548 were heading back to Carlisle coupled together. At 5.20, immediately after the passing of a northbound express, Sutton signalled these two engines out of the yard and onto the down (northbound) main line where they came to a stand at the advanced starter signal. There they would have expected to wait for a minute or two until the express had cleared Ais Gill. In the event they waited 23 minutes.

Sutton managed to forget about them. His attention was taken by other matters. He received the 'train out of section' bell signal from Ais Gill at 5.25 in respect of the northbound express. Instead of offering forward the two Carlisle bound engines, he concentrated on getting the other three light engines on the move. He was also involved in relaying telephone messages to and from enginemen in the yard. A southbound freight went through at 5.29. Sutton saw this as his opportunity to get two light engines away towards Leeds but, immediately, he was offered another southbound freight from Ais Gill. He used the telephone to ask the Ais Gill signalman if he might delay this freight in favour of his light engines but he was prevailed upon to give priority to the freight so he duly accepted it on his block instrument. This second freight trundled past Hawes Junction box at 5.39.

At this stage the overnight express from London St Pancras was rapidly approaching Dent. The train comprised seven bogie vehicles plus a six wheel brake van weighing a total of 378 tons. Though adequately powered with 4-4-0 No. 549 piloted by 2-4-0 No. 48, it was not travelling at excessive speed. The train was 16 minutes late having left Leeds only six minutes behind time.

Dent Box offered this train to Hawes Junction at about 5.40. Signalman Sutton accepted it and immediately offered it on the Ais Gill. Upon acceptance, he 'pulled off' all his down line signals to let it pass.

All this time, drivers Scott and Bath had been waiting patiently at the down advanced starter signal. They should have expected the signal to have been lowered

about 5.25 when the previous train cleared Ais Gill. Under the rules, the fireman of the rear engine should have walked back to the signal box and waited there until the way ahead was clear.

That was the 'official' protection against a train being forgotten about at the starter signal. A further precaution used on some railways was to place a collar on the handle of the home signal lever. This prevented it from being 'pulled' but the Midland Railway declined to issue collars. Some signalmen, including Sutton used ad hoc protectives made of wire but they did not bother with this procedure for light engine movements.

So the scene was set. When at last they saw the arm of the starter signal lower, drivers Scott and Bath assumed that their 23 minute wait had come to an end. Each gave a short blast on the whistle and set off towards Carlisle. It is doubtful that the whistles would have been heard in the signalbox because of the wind. Even if they had, they might have been indistinguishable from sounds coming from engines in the yard.

Meanwhile the express was thundering north under clear signals. The regulators of both engines were fully open. Driver Oldcorn on the (leading) pilot engine was a passed fireman based at Carlisle with plenty of driving experience. He drove through Garsdale Station and across Dandry Mire Viaduct. Then, emerging from Moorcock Tunnel, he saw the tail lamp at the back of the two light engines. Impact followed seconds later.

For his part, driver Bath on the rear light engine, travelling at 25 mph, glanced back and to his horror saw the headlights of the express bearing down on him. He moved swiftly into action, opened up the regulator and sounded the whistle but to no avail.

The impact pushed the two light engines some distance forward of the point where the two train engines came to rest. The two leading coaches telescoped into one another. Almost at once the gas for carriage lighting came into contact with the locomotive coals and there was an explosion. 12 passengers lost their lives.

Major Pringle for the Board of Trade censured Sutton for forgetting about the two light engines saying that he should have noted them in his train register. He recommended that the Midland Railway should issue collars to be placed on the home signal lever when a train or locomotive was standing within station limits.

The drivers of the light engines were also censured for allowing themselves to be forgotten by not despatching a fireman to the signal box nor even by whistling. Ironically, the accident may not have happened under the old signalling arrangements at Hawes Junction since the engines would have been standing much closer to the old North Box than they were to the new one.

In later years track circuiting would have given the signalman a visual indication of the presence of a train within station limits and would also have made it impossible to 'pull off' the home signal.

Ais Gill – 2 September 1913

Two southbound expresses were booked to leave Carlisle at 1.35 and 1.49 am. The first was from Glasgow with a Stranraer portion in the rear. Comprising ten coaches weighing 349 tons, it was hauled by 4-4-0 No. 993 driven by William Nicholson and fired by James Metcalf.

The second train, from Edinburgh, conveyed six 8 wheel carriages weighing a total of 245 tons. At the head

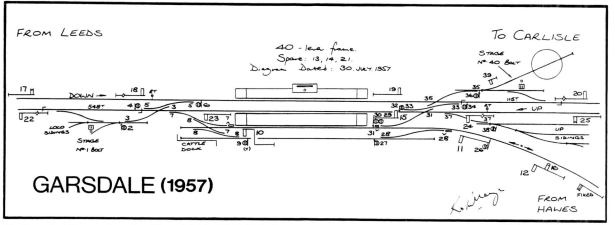

FROM LEEDS

To CARLISLE

40 - lever frame.
Spare: 13, 14, 21.
Diagram Dated: 30 July 1957

STAGE Nº 40 BOLT

DOWN →

UP

LOCO SIDINGS

STAGE Nº 1 BOLT

CATTLE DOCK

UP SIDINGS

UP

GARSDALE (1957)

FROM HAWES

FIXED

The layout at Hawes Junction (Garsdale) in 1957. Little had changed since the alterations earlier in 1910. No 20 is the advance starter. All the signal diagrams are by Richard Pulleyn.

was 4-4-0 No. 446 driven by Samuel Caudle and fired by George Herbert Follows. Caudle had been a driver at Carlisle for 29 years. As a fireman before that he had worked over the Settle & Carlisle line throughout the 37 years since it opened. Follows was not without experience but he was new to this type of engine.

Drivers had been complaining about the quality of a new coal which the Midland Railway had been using at Durran Hill Shed since 1 July 1913. It came from Naworth Colliery, a few miles along the Newcastle line. It was believed to be good locomotive coal if only the colliery would screen it properly.

Before leaving Carlisle, driver Nicholson had asked for a pilot engine but had been told that none was available. This latter fact was later disputed. The only explanation for refusal was that the train was only just over the normal weight for a single loco and it would have taken time to get a pilot loco coupled on.

The 1.35 left Carlisle three minutes late and more or less held time as far as Ormside. Then things became more difficult. Mallerstang Box was passed ten minutes late at about 20 mph with the regulator wide open. The steam pressure was falling rapidly as was the vacuum gauge. The brakes came on and the train drew to a stand just short of the Ais Gill distant signal. Another half mile and it would have reached the summit.

When a train failed in mid section, the guard was supposed to protect it in the rear by placing detonators (fog signals) on the track. The practical drawback was that the subsequent delay in retrieving the guard and the detonators could be longer than the time taken to restore the steam pressure. In any case the train was protected by the block system so crews were reluctant

to use detonators during a short stop. (It would be an entirely different matter if the train was a complete failure because then protection would be needed before an assisting train could be brought into the same block section but that was not the case here).

Guard Donnelly walked up the track to the engine to ask driver Nicholson whether protection was necessary. He was told to return to his van as they would be away again in 'only a few minutes'. Donnelly then made his way to the rear of the train to retail this message to the other guard, Oliver Whitley, who was in charge there.

At this point, Whitley heard the sound of another train approaching from the north. He ran back waving a red lamp but to no avail. His train had been standing for seven minutes when the collision occured.

Meanwhile driver Caudle on No. 446 had pulled out of Carlisle 16 minutes behind Nicholson's train. With the lighter load, he made easier work of the climb from Ormside towards Ais Gill.

After passing Kirkby Stephen under clear signals, the driver left the footplate in order to oil the engine. It was normal procedure for the driver to perform this task on the move, gripping the hand rail as the engine lurched along at 45 mph, with the fireman in charge on the footplate. The Midland Railway had considered banning the practice in 1901 but the Chief Mechanical Engineer had ruled that such a change would be impractical if trains were not to be delayed. Whilst the driver was away, fireman Follows was struggling with the right hand injector on the unfamiliar engine.

Signalman Sutherland at Mallerstang Box had returned all his signals to danger after the first train passed. He accepted the second one from Kirkby

Stephen and shortly afterwards offered it forward to Ais Gill but received no response. He used the telephone to ask whether the first train had yet reached Ais Gill and learnt that it had not. So the signals at Mallerstang remained in the 'on' position.

With the driver groping his way back to the cab and the fireman fighting with the injector, No. 446 sailed past the Mallerstang distant which was at caution.

Signalman Sutherland then made a mistake. He thought that the train had responded to the distant signal and was slowing down for the home so he carried out the normal routine of lowering the home signal slowly. This would indicate that he was only allowing the train to proceed as far as the starter signal where it would have to wait until he had 'line clear' from Ais Gill.

But No. 446 was coming towards Mallerstang Box with its regulator wide open. It passed the home signal in the clear position. Not that either of the engine crew saw it nor did they see the red lamp which signalman Sutherland waved from his box when he realised that the train was approaching too fast to stop nor did they observe the starter signal which was at danger. Caudle and Follows just pressed on past Mallerstang towards Ais Gill.

When fireman Follows did look ahead he saw two red lights. At first he took these to be the Ais Gill distant and home signals. In fact they were the guard's handlamp and the tail lamp of the previous train. His first reaction was to reach for the whistle to warn Ais Gill Box of their approach. Then, as he began to realise

the more urgent significance of the two red lights, he called to the driver who at once shut off steam and applied the brakes. They hit the train in front at about 30 mph.

Signalmen Sutherland at Mallerstang and Clemmet at Ais Gill knew that, unless the first train passed Ais Gill within the next minute or so, there was going to be a collision. Both of them heard the crash and the resultant explosion. Seven minutes later, fireman Metcalf from loco 993 turned up in Ais Gill Box to report it officially.

The gas cut off valves and fire extinguishers introduced after the Hawes Junction accident may have helped but 14 passengers perished at once and another two died later. The Midland Railway claimed to have medical evidence that the first 14 victims died as a result of the impact and not of the fire. Whether the local doctors who came to the scene could really have known that is problematical.

Samuel Caudle was blamed. He was taken off the main line to spend the rest of his working life shunting engines at Durran Hill Shed.

What was really at fault was a system under which drivers were forced to engage in dangerous practices in order not to lose time for which they would be penalised. There was conflicting evidence as to whether the Midland Railway would enforce fines against drivers who had been sent out with bad coal or had been refused a pilot engine for a heavier than normal load. The company said they wouldn't, the National Union of Railwaymen said they did.

No shortage of steam. "Black Fives" 45491 and 44901 approaching Ais Gill with the up "Waverley" on 17 August 1959. *(M Mitchell)*

The Closure Controversy

During 1981, BR announced their intention of diverting the three Nottingham to Glasgow trains via Manchester, away from the Settle & Carlisle line. From May 1982, the remaining Leeds to Carlisle service was reduced to two trains each way, weekdays only. At other times, travellers from Leeds to Carlisle and Glasgow were sent via Lancaster.

About the same time, BR began to leak stories that Ribblehead Viaduct had only five years of life remaining, before a replacement would be needed at prohibitive expense. So began the eight year closure campaign.

At the outset, the line appeared doomed. The outcome in 1989 was the reverse of what had appeared inevitable eight years earlier. A complete transformation had taken place, including an upsurge in passenger traffic generated by the closure threat itself.

Circumstances leading up to the threat of closure

The railway from Settle Junction to Petteril Bridge Junction (Carlisle) is 71 miles in length. It passes through very little population or industry. The largest settlement en route is Appleby, with about 2,000 people.

If BR were concerned at the cost of maintaining these 71 heavily engineered miles, there was a simple alternative. Just revert to the position which would have applied if the 1869 Abandonment Bill had been passed.

The Ingleton route was two miles shorter overall and involved only 23 miles of self contained track between Clapham and Low Gill. And it served Penrith whose traffic potential is surely greater than all the places on the Settle & Carlisle line combined.

The local passenger service between Clapham and Low Gill was withdrawn in January 1954 but the double track remained open for a small volume of local freight, for special trains to Sedbergh and Barbon at the beginning and end of school terms and for traffic diverted off the Settle & Carlisle in emergencies.

It is believed that BR did consider closure of the Settle & Carlisle in favour of Ingleton but such tentative ideas were completely overtaken by the 1963 Beeching Report. This recommended closure of the Settle & Carlisle line with provision that the alternative route should be abandoned first.

The Ingleton route had no booked traffic after February 1965 but it remained available as a diversionary route until June 1966. Track lifting took place during 1967 and then they began to sell off bits of the formation.

Meanwhile, BR had issued a formal closure proposal in respect of the local service between Hellifield and Carlisle. This move was refused by the Minister of Transport in November 1964 on the grounds of hardship to users. This was a token reprieve on a day when the Minister approved 40 other closures, some of them affecting far more passengers than this.

Hardship to users was forgotten when the Minister approved a renewed application for closure. The local trains were withdrawn in May 1970, leaving Appleby as the only station open between Settle and Carlisle. There remained three passenger trains a day, one of them in the middle of the night.

It was expected that complete closure of the Settle & Carlisle would take some time. First it would be required as a diversionary route during electrification of the West Coast Main Line. This was authorised in 1970 and completed in 1974. But they removed all the catch points on the main line, meaning that Settle & Carlisle was still required for unfitted freight.

Since 1889, it had been compulsory for passenger trains to have automatic continuous brakes. But it had been thought impossible to equip all the thousands of goods wagons. Many freight trains still ran unfitted

For the last three years until closure in 1970, the local service was DMU operated and the stations were unstaffed. A class 113 Cravens Hydraulic unit calls at Dent, bound for Skipton.
(Martin Bairstow collection)

or partially fitted. If a coupling broke between two unfitted vehicles on an uphill gradient, the rear portion would have only the guard's handbrake. To prevent it running back into a following train, there had to be catch points to derail runaways.

The decline in traditional wagon load traffic was rapidly bringing an end to unfitted freight working. By 1981, the Settle & Carlisle was no longer indispensable for its catch points.

1975 saw a very limited revival of local trains. Chartered by the Yorkshire Dales National Park and marketed as Dales Rail, the service ran one weekend per month, about a dozen operating days a year. It carried about 5,000 passengers annually – less than some lines carry in an hour – but achieved a publicity value out of proportion.

From May 1977, the Leeds – Glasgow service was improved to give three day time trains each way, all through from Nottingham. For the first time it was practical to get from Carlisle to Leeds and back in the same day. By way of compensation, the overnight train ceased to carry passengers.

Friends of the Settle – Carlisle Line
By the Autumn of 1981, the outlook appeared very bleak. Freight was in terminal decline. The express passenger service was to be diverted away. The limited Dales Rail operation showed no sign of developing any further. There were only two intermediate stations open on a regular basis. Settle had the option of a more frequent service at Giggleswick. Appleby saw about 50 passengers a day.

It was against this background that "Friends of the Settle – Carlisle Line" was formed. One of the founders was Graham Nuttall who became the first Secretary. He was a regular user of the line, invariably accompanied by his border collie dog named Ruswarp. Sadly in January 1990, Graham suffered a fall whilst on a walking holiday in Wales. He was discovered weeks later having died of exposure. The

event caught the attention of the national press, mainly because of the survival of Ruswarp who had remained faithfully at the scene.

From modest beginnings, the "Friends" went on to play a major part in the campaign to secure the future of the line. The Association is still in being with over 3,000 members. It continues to campaign for improvements, to raise funds and help with publicity. It also provides the volunteer workforce, which has done so much to improve the local stations and which has established a pattern for similar initiative elsewhere on the network.

Other players in the campaign
The Settle – Carlisle Joint Action Committee was an amalgam of the "Friends", the Railway Development Society and the union sponsored Transport 2000. Its main function seemed to be the issue of an unending series of press statements. It didn't seem to gain the same respect as the "Friends" and disbanded after the line was saved.

Throughout the campaign, the "Friends" and Joint Action Committee enjoyed the support of local MPs, both Government and Opposition.

Absolutely crucial were the local authorities. They provided finance for the improvement in service which proved a turning point in the fight to save the line. The prime mover was Cumbria County Council, which brought North Yorkshire and Lancashire County Councils and the West Yorkshire Passenger Transport Executive, together with all relevant District Councils into a Joint Councils Steering Group.

The Press played a key role. There were sympathetic editors and journalists in most of the local papers. There was quite a bit of national coverage as well.

There were also plenty of individuals who made their voices heard during the eight years.

On the BR side, there was Ron Cotton who was appointed in October 1983 as project manager for the

Graham Nuttall's dog "Ruswarp" receives the RSPCA's highest accolade in Burnley on 28 September 1990.
(Burnley Express)

31226 crossing Ais Gill Viaduct with the afternoon Carlisle to Leeds on 29 May 1982, shortly after the service was reduced to twice a day. *(Tom Heavyside)*

Settle & Carlisle Line. His brief was to close it. Yet he promoted it so as to quadruple the number of passengers during the period it was under threat. He was a marketing man at the end of his career. It might have been different had they given the job to a young executive hungry for promotion.

The Transport Users Consultative Committees
These bodies were originally constituted under the Transport Act 1948. They served as a kind of tribunal to approve railway closures. In the 1950s, most closures attracted little or no opposition. Where they did, the Committees sometimes declined or delayed approval. In that form, they might have posed a threat to the programme of mass closures envisaged by Dr Beeching and his political master Ernest Marples. So the 1962 Act changed their role just to gather information and report to the Minister of Transport on the one subject of hardship. The decision was for the Minister alone. Initially that meant Ernest Marples, the very architect of the closure policy.

The 1962 legislation lasted until privatisation in the 1990s. From the early 1970s, there were very few closures and some area TUCCs never had to deal with one. Instead they acted as a kind of consumer watchdog.

Mr James Towler was appointed as CBI representative on the Yorkshire Area TUCC in 1973. He became Chairman in 1979. He was not a person to be Chairman of anything without making his presence felt. He did more than anyone to create public awareness of these rather impotent committees.

It so happened that the Yorkshire Area had more than its share of closure proposals in a period when the size of the BR network was more or less stable. Some were of marginal significance – the short Saturdays only branch to Filey Holiday Camp and the Hull to New Holland Ferry, whose demise was inevitable when the Humber Bridge opened. Later there were the Goole - Gilberdyke and Huddersfield – Penistone proposals. In both these cases, the TUCC managed to create delay, sufficient to enable a local authority rescue package to appear.

Settle & Carlisle was the big one. From 1981, Mr Towler advised the anti-closure lobby on procedures. He fought off an attempt to have the matter dealt with exclusively by the North West TUCC which appeared to take a more neutral stance. When he was relieved of his responsibilities in 1987, he became Chairman of the Yorkshire branch of the Railway Development Society, which he tried to turn into a kind of shadow TUCC.

The Phoney War
The first two years of the campaign were spent waiting for something to happen. The Nottingham to Glasgow trains were diverted in May 1982. They were replaced between Leeds and Carlisle by two trains each way, daily except Sundays, on the most inefficient rosters which involved crews working a single Skipton to Carlisle single trip per shift. In addition, three Leeds to Morecambe trains were accelerated by missing intermediate stops then diverted via Lancaster where they offered connections to Carlisle and Glasgow.

Several times, BR denied that any decision had been taken to close the Settle & Carlisle line. This stance was repeated in letters to MPs from officials as high as the BR Chairman Sir Peter Parker. Nobody believed them, particular in view of a leaked "confidential" memo which fell into the hands of the "Friends".

In October 1982, the overnight mail and parcels trains were diverted via Carnforth allowing the night shift to be abolished at signal boxes between Settle Junction and Carlisle.

On 13 May 1983, the last through freight, the 14.20

Carlisle to Healey Mills was hauled by loco No 40196. This left just one local freight, daily if required, from Carlisle to Appleby.

During this period, the "Friends" and Joint Action Committee managed to generate public interest including coverage on television. Finally in August 1983, BR published a five year corporate plan, giving the first official confirmation that closure was intended.

The Closure Proceedings
Things then began to move. Ron Cotton was appointed to oversee closure in October. Then in December, the formal notice was published to close the railway between Settle Junction and Petteril Bridge Junction (Carlisle), to close Settle and Appleby Stations and to divert the Leeds – Carlisle trains via Carnforth with stops at Giggleswick and Penrith. A seven week period was allowed for objections.

The total number received by the Yorkshire and North West TUCCs was a rather disappointing 2,369. By comparison, the concurrent proposal to close the seven mile link between Goole and Gilberdyke generated 2,485. Thus far, the Settle & Carlisle performance was verging on an anti climax. The closure notice had specified only the regular timetabled trains calling at Settle and Appleby. This

had not dissuaded customers of Dales Rail and other excursions from having their say. The TUCCs accepted all objections and refused a request that BR might have sight of them, presumably to check their authenticity.

The Small Print
Early in 1984, the Secretary of the Yorkshire TUCC noticed a discrepancy between the wording of the closure notice and that of the 1962 Act. Every closure notice since 1962 had invited objections from "any user of the service which it is proposed to discontinue". What the Act said was "any user of any service affected".

Users of Dales Rail and steam excursions had, at least in theory, been denied their opportunity. So had people who boarded the 7.39 Settle to Leeds at Long Preston, Hellifield and Gargrave.

Reluctantly BR conceded, announcing in April 1984 that a revised notice would be issued widening the scope for objections and including eight Dales Rail stations plus Clitheroe on the Blackburn to Hellifield line which was used on about six days a year. It was made clear that previous objections still counted and did not need repeating.

The second seven week period in May to July 1984 saw the number of Goole to Gilberdyke

A class 123/124 hybrid set on a Leeds – Lancaster – Morecambe "express" accelerates away from Settle Junction on 7 April 1984. *(G W Morrison)*

objections rise from 2,485 to 2,570. By contrast, the tally for Settle & Carlisle went up from 2,369 to 11,117. The "Friends" had become better organised. Members had been handing out pro formas on the trains, then collecting them for bulk delivery to the TUCC.

The pretext for having a third objection period was much more fanciful. A short section of line near Ais Gill, which included no stations, lay within the Area covered by the North East TUCC who had not been mentioned in either the first or second notices. The North East TUCC itself was unenthusiastic but, amazingly, BR conceded and issued the closure notice a third time.

The machinery for collecting objections just continued for a further seven week period. The cumulative total was brought up to 22,150 of which a mere 69 were sent to the North East Committee in Newcastle. By a huge margin, this was an all time record for any railway closure. The overwhelming majority of objections were on pro-formas handed out on trains, many of them from people making their once ever journey on the line. Hundreds gave overseas addresses and one was claimed to be from a dog. Nobody knows the extent of duplication – the same person objecting from different accommodation addresses, writing to both or even

all three TUCCs, availing of all three objection periods.

The Settle & Carlisle lobby had won the numbers game. "22,000 and a dog" was all the press wanted to know. Substance and authenticity didn't matter.

In July 1984, Ron Cotton scored his first marketing initiative. For the remainder of the summer, there was a third Leeds – Carlisle return train each weekday plus the first timetabled Sunday train since May 1982.

A special fare offer during the early part of 1985 led to the morning Leeds – Carlisle train having to be duplicated on Saturdays. On 30 March, it was triplicated. The usual double headed class 31 + ten coaches was followed by a class 47 + nine, then by a six car DMU.

Mr Towler, meanwhile was fighting internal battles. First he sought to prevent the North West TUCC from taking control of the issue. The greater part of the threatened line was in their area but the Yorkshire Committee had received two thirds of the objections. The North West Committee were proposing to stick to the traditional view that only considerations of hardship were relevant. A compromise was struck whereby the two bodies would hold public hearings at their respective ends of the line but issue a joint report.

Then the Government came up with a plan to

47475 south of Rise Hill Tunnel with the 12.42 from Carlisle to Leeds on 16 August 1988.

(David A Smith)

redraw the TUCC area boundaries. The Yorkshire Area would merge with the North East under the chairmanship of Mr Towler but would cede the Craven District (Skipton – Ribblehead) to the North West thereby giving them sole jurisdiction of the Settle & Carlisle matter. Somehow, Mr Towler managed to retain the Craven District for the North East.

The public hearings were held over a total of 16 non consecutive days in March and April 1986 beginning on a snowy day in Appleby and proceeding via Carlisle, Settle and Skipton to Leeds. TUCC members stayed in hotels, even when in easy reach of home.

Normally, BR would have been represented by one or more senior officers. Legal representation was unheard of. This time, the three seats at the BR table were occupied by Ron Cotton, Michael Harrison QC and his instructing solicitor. The QC appeared to be there solely to give Mr Cotton permission to answer questions.

Mr Towler assumed the chair from Settle onwards with such impartiality that he referred to the BR solicitor as a tea boy.

Of the 392 objectors or representatives who spoke, very few could claim dependence on the line for essential journeys. The service just didn't lend itself. Quite a few Dales Rail patrons said the train afforded access to the countryside but this applied on only half a dozen weekends a year. Otherwise Mr Towler was having to clutch at straws. The eventual TUCC report referred to hardship to aficionados of locomotive No D200.

It was left to Ron Cotton to add a bit of substance to the anti-closure case. He announced that "due to pathing difficulties", the rerouted morning Leeds – Carlisle train would stand over half an hour in the down goods loop at Carnforth during which time passengers would be exhorted not to use the loos.

Local Stations re-opened

Aware of the limitations of the existing train service, the local authorities announced at the public hearings that they were prepared to offer financial support for a more comprehensive local service. Ron Cotton confirmed that BR were ready to discuss such a thing on a charter basis, for as long as the line remained open. Mr Harrison QC confirmed that it would be a charter arrangement not in the public timetable.

Things moved remarkably quickly, once the hearings were over. Monday 14 July 1986 saw the reopening to normal traffic of the eight stations used hitherto only by Dales Rail. They were served by a DMU running twice a day from Skipton to Carlisle and back. The first northbound and last southbound trips were timed for commuters into Carlisle from Kirkby Stephen, Appleby and the Eden Valley. The express trains also made one or two extra stops. The local authorities gave revenue support and paid for new station lighting. It was not a charter service, but part of the normal timetable.

Some members of the anti-closure lobby were apprehensive. The local trains had been poorly patronised prior to withdrawal in 1970. If this initiative failed, it might be the end of the fight. Thanks to the mid summer start and good publicity, patronage began well.

By September 1986, the Councils had declared themselves well pleased and had agreed financial support for a modified service to continue from May 1987. This merged the existing express and local services to give five trains a day, all through from Leeds serving most stations north from Settle.

With BR still intent on closing and demolishing it, Friends of the Settle – Carlisle Line give Horton in Ribblesdale its first coat of paint for many years in August 1987.

(Martin Bairstow)

Local trains restored. A class 108 DMU in original green livery apart from the yellow ends, deposits customers at Kirkby Stephen on 4 October 1986. The TUCC Report said nothing about hardship to users of this revived service.
(Martin Bairstow)

It did, however, plead the cause of followers of D200. Built in 1958, the pioneer class 40 was withdrawn in 1981 but reinstated in 1983. For the next five years, it sometimes worked the morning Carlisle – Leeds. It is seen at Skipton.
(Martin Bairstow collection)

Towards a decision

At the end of 1986, the TUCCs presented a very weighty report to the Secretary of State for Transport. Needless to say, they recommended against closure "strongly and emphatically". The report scarcely mentioned the revived local service, which had introduced a number of travellers who now depended on the train for journeys to work and college. The omission may have been deliberate, to provoke a re-run in the event of an adverse Ministerial decision. Or it may have been sheer idleness on the part of the TUCCs. The published report was made up largely of recycled material from the Joint Action Committee and others given at the time of the public hearings.

Made public at the same time was the BR financial case for closure. Speaking as a Chartered Accountant, I can say that this read like nonsense. Costs of maintaining a Leeds to Carlisle service via Settle were weighted heavily by depreciation on Sprinter DMUs.

But if the service were rerouted via Carnforth, these trains were apparently free.

The Press took up stories denouncing the BR financial case but these often owed more to journalistic licence than technical input. But the "Friends" had the expertise and contacts with which to communicate at the appropriate level.

Attention began to focus on the local authorities. It seemed doubtful that BR would re-close the local stations, which had reopened with quite a measure of success. Elsewhere in the Country, they were trying to encourage this sort of initiative, with local authority support.

David Mitchell MP was junior Minister with responsibility for public transport for a comparatively long tenure of five years, 1983 to 1988. He began to take an interest in the Settle & Carlisle issue. He received a lot of lobbying, much of it quite professional from the Councils and from the

"Friends". He asked how much support the local authorities would guarantee.

Cumbria County Council and various District Councils pledged their share towards a £½m target. West Yorkshire PTE joined on the grounds that loss of the Carlisle trains would increase the cost of the remaining subsidised local service in Airedale and Wharfedale. Last to fall in line was North Yorkshire County Council. With a £15,000 pledge from the "Friends", Mr Mitchell's target was reached.

By the Spring of 1988, the way seemed clear for a Government decision in favour of retention. One can only suppose that David Mitchell himself was not the brains behind the announcement which he made in the House of Commons on 16 May 1988. He left the Government three months later.

He informed the House that the Secretary of State was "minded" to agree the closure but would delay a final decision for six months pending a supplementary report from the TUCCs. It would then consider transferring the line to the private sector.

The last lap

At that time, railway privatisation was nothing more than a distant ambition of the Conservative Party. Some politicians described the growing number of preserved or Heritage lines as "private railways". BR had steadfastly resisted any of these running over its tracks. They had recently placed insurmountable obstacles in the way of the North Yorkshire Moors Railway extending to Whitby, something which has happened more recently under a different regime.

Were the Government contemplating Settle & Carlisle as a test bed for privatisation or were they merely saying that the redundant railway might become a heritage operation confined to some stretch between Settle and Armathwaite?

People asked whether a privatised Settle & Carlisle would be allowed to link into the national network. Speaking on radio, David Mitchell said there should be no problem as BR and a "private" railway already shared tracks at Alton, near his constituency. This was nonsense. I told him, face to face on Garsdale Station, that the tracks at Alton are as segregated as those at Keighley. He said I would have to write to his office if I wanted an answer to my "question".

BR issued a "prospectus", offering the line for sale, or give away. It didn't specify which. It didn't say much at all, except to confirm that running outside of Settle or Petteril Bridge Junctions would be subject to the same impossible conditions which blocked it

47475 has just emerged from Blea Moor Tunnel with the 8.25 am from Leeds to Carlisle on 16 August 1988. *(David A Smith)*

between Grosmont and Whitby. The document came out with one incredible statement. As the line was operated as an integral part of the BR network, it was not possible to establish the traffic or revenue or costs directly attributable to it. Had the BR case for closure been made up? Or was the author of this latest document just too idle to read it? Or was the Prospectus being deliberately made to look ridiculous?

The TUCCs, now under new management, declined to support calls for a full re-run of the closure procedure. There were now people using the line for essential journeys which had not existed when the closure was first announced. BR had omitted to issue a notice bringing the revived local service under the "Speller Amendment", which allowed a new service to be declared an experiment and exempted from the statutory closure process should they subsequently wish to withdraw it.

BR said that the stations had all been included in the closure notice and that a service of five trains a day was merely a timetable change from the dozen or so charter trains per annum. The TUCCs agreed. Instead, they invited the public to send them updated information about journeys so they could report to the Government on what buses would be required to replace the trains.

At a speech in Carlisle, David Mitchell confirmed that rail replacement buses from the Beeching Period had been "here today and gone tomorrow" but promised that those for future rail closures would be "guaranteed". There had been no buses before the local trains resumed and patrons were not likely to transfer to any if the trains were withdrawn again. But the TUCCs did their best to devise bus journeys which might shadow the trains.

The consultative machinery under the 1962 Act had been designed to permit closure of half the BR network over a very short period. It did not allow for marathons. There was no precedent for traffic to quadruple or for stations to reopen on a line passing through the closure system. Nobody knew whether a decision to close would be subject to legal challenge, nor what if anything was meant by the Government's talk of privatisation.

Autumn 1988 came and went without the six month delayed decision. The councils, "Friends" and others continued to lobby. According to press reports, negotiations were taking place with two East Yorkshire businessmen who had formed a company called Cumbrian Railways Ltd to take over the line. Actually they had also formed Ribblehead Viaduct Ltd and Rail Leisure Ltd but it costs next to nothing to form a company.

The Councils said they would work with the private sector to keep the railway open. Equally they would be prepared to discuss a joint approach with BR and a charitable trust. Then, quite unexpectedly, on Tuesday 11 April 1989, it was announced by Michael Portillo MP that the Secretary of State had refused consent to closure.

In a press release which read as though it had been prepared for an adverse decision, the Department of Transport again rejected the TUCCs findings and confirmed that "guaranteed" buses would be quite adequate for the needs of the community. However, since the cost of repairs was now less than expected, the line would stay open.

BR welcomed the decision which left one wondering what the eight year fight had been about in the first place.

47770 drags driving trailer 82104 past Hellifield with the 10.25 Euston to Glasgow on 22 January 2000.
(Tom Heavyside)

After 1989

During the period of threatened closure, the Settle & Carlisle line had been exempt from the changes which were rapidly transforming travel on other non Inter City routes. The ten coach loco hauled trains had begun to stand out when policy elsewhere was in favour of short "Sprinter" and "Pacer" DMUs.

As soon as the reprieve was announced, BR prepared for the introduction of class 156 "sprinters". These might have started with the May 1990 timetable, but late delivery of the 158s had a knock on effect, which saw the class 47 locos replaced by smaller 31s hauling shorter trains which were allowed three hours for the 113 miles. The "sprinters" started on 1 October 1990 on the same schedule causing extended station stops en route. The timetable was eventually tightened up to give a typical journey time of 2¾ hours.

Meanwhile work had already begun to catch up arrears of maintenance. The line was closed between Settle and Appleby for two weeks at the end of October 1989, whilst work was carried out on Ribblehead Viaduct and other structures.

After a number of setbacks, the "Friends" put together a financial package to provide the missing platform at Ribblehead. This comprised grants from various agencies including the "Friends" themselves. Trains were able to stop in both directions from 28 May 1993.

At the reopened stations, some of the buildings had been demolished or sold out of railway use. Those which remained had fallen into disrepair. Gradually, during the 1990s, each platform was equipped with a shelter, comprising the original Midland building where still available. All the stations, including Settle and Appleby were provided with electric lighting in the style of traditional gas or oil lamps.

Historically, each station had a clock, a vital tool when engine crews tended not to carry watches and few passengers had them. Usually, the clockwork mechanism was inside the ticket office with a second face on the platform side. Accuracy was checked with the daily time signal on the telegraph.

Being better cared for than many stations, Settle and Appleby had retained their clocks but those at the other stations had disappeared. In 2005, the derelict time piece at Kirkby Stephen was restored. This led to the acquisition of five new clocks, which were fitted in the vacant holes at Horton, Ribblehead, Dent, Langwathby and Lazonby. They were supplied by Potts of Leeds, long standing makers of station clocks. The new ones are driven by electricity, the absence of which has prevented an installation at Garsdale, The scheme was defeated at Armathwaite by the hole in the wall having been filled in.

Starting in 1987, volunteers had begun some maintenance and gardening work on the eight unstaffed stations. At first this was revolutionary,

156438 calls at Garsdale on 12 September 1998. *(Tom Heavyside)*

156 489 deposits a handful of walkers at the new northbound platform at Ribblehead on 5 June 1993.
(Martin Bairstow)

156 489 leaving Ribblehead for Carlisle on 30 May 1998. The siding in the foreground caused demolition of the original down platform.
(Tom Heavyside)

tolerated but not really encouraged by BR. Later on, particularly after privatisation, the arrangement became an established part of the Settle & Carlisle operation, and has spread to other routes.

11 October 1999 saw the start of a through service from Leeds to Glasgow at 9.47am. Worked by a class 158, it went by the Caledonian Main Line from Carlisle. It finished on 27 September 2003 on the pretext that the class 158 would be a liability if it broke down between Carlisle and Glasgow. There was no actual experience of this happening.

For the next 12 months, the 9.47 departure was still not without interest. There was another fortnight's engineering blockage so it was not until 13 October 2003 that it resumed as four Mark 2 coaches with a class 37 loco on each end. These worked in multiple making for a high powered train which was more comfortable and spacious than the DMUs. It performed a trip to Carlisle and back in between its rush hour diagram from Knaresborough into Leeds. On Saturdays, it ran from York to Carlisle and back. To the regret of many, it finished on 25 September 2004.

The 156s gave way to 158s when these were released by Trans Pennine in 2007. They are sometimes strengthened by single car 153s. On weekdays, there are seven trains each way between Leeds and Carlisle plus one between Leeds and Ribblehead. On Sundays there are three between Leeds and Carlisle. Summer only at one time, the Sunday service became year round in 1998.

The Return of Freight

This has been the most significant development since the 1989 reprieve.

Regular freight resumed in November 1993 when BR gained a contract to move desulphogypsum from Drax power station to the British Gypsum plant at Kirkby Thore. The material is a by product of the power station's gas desulperisation process which reduces sulphur dioxide emissions. The initial contract was for up to five train loads per week. The traffic is still running, having fluctuated over the years between two trains a day and periods without.

In former times Kirkby Thore had been accessed from a ground frame but for the new traffic they commissioned a new signal box.

The mid 1990s saw further contraction in the domestic coal industry. This produced new movements of coal from Scotland to the remaining coal fired power stations. Much of the coal is imported via Hunterston, on the Largs branch. By 1997, there were up to 56 coal trains a week passing over the Settle & Carlisle line. But for many years the track had been maintained for a passenger only, largely DMU operation. It wasn't up to the increased strain.

This was demonstrated rather spectacularly on 14 July 1998, when a loaded coal train derailed. Loco No 60 085 came to a stand on Dent Head Viaduct, with only the first three wagons still on the track. The next three stayed upright. The remaining 29 ended all over the place, some down the embankment. Thanks to

60083 passing Kirkby Stephen with Kirkby Thore to Drax empties on 12 April 2007.　*(Tom Heavyside)*

37405 brings up the rear of the 9.47 Leeds – Carlisle on 12 April 2004. For a short time, the 40 year old engines and 30 year old carriages were the best train on the line. *(Martin Bairstow)*

66241 passing Garsdale with gypsum empties on 14 February 2001. *(Tom Heavyside)*

the remote location and that no train was coming the other way, there were no casualties. The line was closed for nearly a fortnight. The accident prompted a major track renewal programme which lasted several years involving a lot of fortnight long closures.

The freight revival also exposed the inadequacy of the signalling system. The run down had seen closure of many of the signal boxes. By 1984, normal working was Settle Junction – Blea Moor – Kirkby Stephen – Culgaith – Low House Crossing – Howe & Cos Siding, giving block sections between 14 and 18 miles, apart from the last one which was only three miles. It would have required investment to close one or other of these last two boxes. Either they would have had to automate the level crossing at Low House or they would have had to extend the track circuits so that Low House could fringe on to Carlisle power box.

Garsdale and Appleby boxes didn't close but were kept switched out, except in emergencies. The resumption of freight caused them to reopen permanently and for all the boxes to go back on to 24 hour working. There still remained two long sections which were finally split in 2008 with the provision of intermediate block signals at Horton and Lazonby.

The loaded coal trains run southbound so four additional intermediate block signals were erected on the up line only at Ormside, Crosby Garrett, Mallerstang and Ais Gill to shorten further the sections on the ascent to Ais Gill Summit.

The Automatic Warning System was installed in 1997, at which time the remaining semaphore distant signals were replaced by colour lights. The system gives the driver an audible warning on the approach to a signal which is showing red or yellow. He must acknowledge the warning or there is an automatic brake application. It was first introduced on BR in 1956, but took over 40 years to reach the Settle & Carlisle line.

On 13 August 2010, the line gained a second source of intermediate freight when 47 739 "Robin of Templecombe" left Ribblehead with the first load of timber destined for Chirk.

Coach Parties
Preserved or heritage railways try to sell themselves to tour operators who bring a bus load of patrons for a ride on a steam train, sometimes in one direction only, the bus shadowing the train. As we read in *Railways in Mallorca*, this is big business on the Soller Railway, whose electric trains date from 1929. It is very rare for this class of trade to be seen on a part of the national network operated by normal diesel trains.

The phenomenon is something which arose out of the publicity surrounding the closure threat. There is a steady traffic in coach parties who are often conveyed for a single journey between Settle and Appleby.

The business, though welcome, is not without problems. Some of the trains have only two carriages. When all or most of one is reserved for the

66199 passing through Carlisle Station with up coal on 19 March 2001. *(Tom Heavyside)*

coach party, there can be insufficient room for ordinary passengers. On a recent journey, the guard removed the reservation labels to make room for passengers joining at Keighley and Skipton. On arrival at Settle, the train was already full. Passengers joining there, both booked party and individuals, had to stand in pretty uncomfortable conditions. Seeing the scrum, I got off at Settle and waited an hour for the next train, a four car with plenty of room.

Blackburn to Hellifield

The formal decision by the Secretary of State to refuse closure even applied to the half dozen or so trains a year using the Blackburn to Hellifield line and calling at Clitheroe. It was this tenuous connection which had enabled Lancashire County Council to play a small part in the Settle & Carlisle campaign.

The regular passenger service had been withdrawn in September 1962 but the route had continued for freight and emergency diversions in connection with the Settle & Carlisle. By the 1980s, it had very little regular traffic.

From May 1990, with County Council support, a limited service ran from Blackburn to Clitheroe on Summer Saturdays. At the same time, a Summer Sunday train was introduced all the way to Carlisle. In May 1994, Blackburn to Clitheroe reopened on a more substantial basis with an hourly service and three intermediate stations. North of Clitheroe, there continues just the Summer Sunday train.

The Clitheroe revival was arguably an extension of the successful Settle & Carlisle campaign.

Wensleydale

Success in saving the Settle & Carlisle line caused some people to turn their attention along the Hawes branch. The track bed lies abandoned in many different ownerships but largely free from obstruction all the way through Hawes, Askrigg and Aysgarth to Redmire.

The Wensleydale Railway Association was formed in 1990 with the bold object of reinstating 19 miles between Garsdale and Redmire and eventual operation all the way to Northallerton.

During 1992, the Association found itself fighting an unsuccessful campaign to head off closure of the remaining Redmire to Northallerton section. First, British Steel said they were going to divert the stone traffic to road because BR had raised its price. Then, just as a solution seemed possible, they announced that Redmire Quarry was to be closed and stone obtained instead from Shap with rail haulage (a much longer journey) to their plant on Teesside.

The 22 mile line closed on 2 January 1993. But then it reopened for occasional use by the army delivering tanks to Redmire for transfer to Catterick. With this traffic still in place, the line was sold to the Wensleydale Railway who began a heritage operation in 2003 between Leyburn and Leeming Bar. The following year they extended back to Redmire but have yet to establish a link with the national network by filling the gap between Leeming Bar and Northallerton. It remains their ambition eventually to rebuild west from Redmire towards Garsdale.

60090 approaching Ais Gill with gypsum empties on 21 October 1997.   *(Tom Heavyside)*

Closed to regular passenger trains in 1962, the Blackburn to Hellifield survived in connection with the Settle & Carlisle Line. Class 47 No D1857 passing the 1911 signal box at Hellifield South Junction with the diverted "Royal Scot" on 16 August 1967.
(Martin Bairstow collection)

The reopening of Clitheroe on 29 May 1994 was a further result of the Settle & Carlisle campaign. 150 150 offloads passengers from Blackburn on 9 July that year.
(Martin Bairstow)

The Wensleydale project also flowed from the Settle & Carlisle business. Class 107 Nos 52006+59791+52025 at Redmire on 29 August 2004.
(Martin Bairstow)

The Return of Steam

Sunday 11 August 1968 saw crowds thronging the lineside to witness the passing of the "Fifteen Guinea Special" which made its way from Liverpool Lime Street to Carlisle and back via Manchester, Blackburn and Settle. It was hauled from Manchester to Carlisle by No 70013 "Oliver Cromwell", returning with two "black fives", Nos 44871 and 44781. It was supposed to be the last steam train ever on British Railways. As BR pointed out, to allow any further steam operation would be to commit fraud on those who had paid fifteen guineas to be on the last one.

Less than four years later, BR published a list of routes over which steam charter trains would be permitted. These included Leeds to Carnforth and Newcastle to Carlisle but steam remained banned over the Settle & Carlisle line even for its centenary celebrations on 1 May 1976.

BR was finally persuaded to give way in 1978, allowing class V2 No 4771 "Green Arrow" to haul the first steam charter for nearly ten years over the Settle & Carlisle on 25 March.

Since then, occasional steam trains have been a regular feature on the Settle & Carlisle Line. As a general rule, tours operate over quite a long distance, sometimes covering the Settle & Carlisle in one direction only. By way of example, on 14 June 2012, the "Cumbrian Mountain Express" starts at London Euston with class 86 electric haulage to Preston. It continues with steam to Carlisle, out via Blackburn and Settle and back over the West Coast Main Line. On four dates later in the year, a different "Cumbrian Mountain Express" is steam hauled from Crewe to Carlisle, out by the Main Line and back via Settle.

Every Sunday from 22 July to 9 September, the "Waverley" goes from York to Carlisle and back, steam hauled both ways via Settle. The "Fellsman", every Wednesday from 4 July to 29 August, goes from Lancaster to Carlisle picking up at Preston, Blackburn, Clitheroe and Long Preston, steam all the way returning by the same route. The trains are aimed at a variety of markets, offering first and second class plus dining options.

A problem with steam operation is the need to stop and take water en route, sometimes from road tankers at Hellifield, Long Preston or Garsdale. In 1991, a rather more authentic water tower and column were brought into use at the south end of Appleby Station following fund raising by the local round table.

Similar charter trains also run with diesel locomotives. On four consecutive Saturdays in May and June 2012, the "Settle & Carlisle Statesman" starts at around 6am from Bristol Temple Meads, Newport (Gwent), Peterborough or Cambridge, for a trip to Carlisle and back.

4 – 6 – 2 No 46229 "Duchess of Hamilton" approaching Blea Moor with the northbound "Cumbrian Mountain Express" on 29 October 1983. Originally steamlined, the "Coronation" class were built for the West Coast Main Line. They appeared occasionally on the Settle & Carlisle line in emergencies.
(Tom Heavyside)

5407 passing Keld with a Carlisle to Wakefield special on 12 September 1998.   *(Tom Heavyside)*

"Deltic" No D9009 "Alycidon" passing Garsdale with a Carlisle to York charter on 15 September 1999.
(Tom Heavyside)

"Jubilee" class 4 – 6 – 0 No 5593 "Kolhapur" passing Gargrave with an excursion from York to Carlisle
on 21 March 1987. *(Tom Heavyside)*

Midland compound 4 – 4 – 0 No 1000, of 1902, pilots No 5690 "Leander" of 1936, just north of Culgaith,
with the southbound "Cumbrian Mountain Pullman" on 12 February 1983. *(Tom Heavyside)*

Opening and Closure Dates

Opened

Leeds – Shipley	30/06/1846
Shipley – Keighley	16/03/1847
Keighley – Skipton	07/09/1847
Skipton – Settle Junction	30/07/1849
Settle Jn – Stainforth (goods)	1873
Stainforth - Petteril Br Jn (goods)	02/08/1875
Settle Jn – Petteril Br Jn (passr)	01/05/1876
Petteril Bridge Jn – Carlisle	01/01/1863
Garsdale – Hawes (goods)	01/08/1878
Garsdale – Hawes (passenger)	01/10/1878

Closed

Garsdale – Hawes	14/03/1959

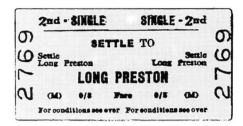

Distinctly Midland in appearance, the Joint Station at Hawes opened to passengers on 1 October 1878 and closed on 14 March 1959.
(Martin Bairstow collection)

There was a short delay in determining sites for Ribblehead and Dent Stations. They opened respectively on 4 December 1876 and 6 August 1877. The remoteness of Dent, looking south.
(Martin Bairstow collection)

Conclusion

The Settle & Carlisle Line need never have been built. The Ingleton route offered a perfectly good alternative. In the era of railway closures, they could easily have got rid of Settle & Carlisle in favour of Ingleton.

Instead, they chose to destroy Ingleton before beginning the run down of Settle & Carlisle. Then they embarked on a botched scheme to try and close it. Publicity surrounding the Closure Campaign is one of the reasons why the line is now as busy as ever.

Half a century after being written off in the Beeching Report, Ribblehead has more passengers than ever before.
(Martin Bairstow collection)

Traditional wagonload freight has gone. 8F 2 – 8 – 0 No 48464 approaching Ais Gill with an up freight on 13 May 1961.
(J C W Halliday collection)

But trainload freight has returned. 66035 passing Ais Gill with northbound coal empties on 13 July 2002.
(Tom Heavyside)

Book Review

Tunnels of the Southern

This is an impressive book, which is nevertheless hard to classify. Published by the well respected Railway Tunnel Historical Society, it comprises large size colour photographs taken inside all the major and most minor tunnels on the former Southern Railway system. Having said this, however, the colour is almost wholly black, for the photographs have been taken under conditions of authenticity – and most RTHS excursions can in any case only be held at night when traffic conditions allow. No artificial lighting was used, as this would detract from the authenticity – such are the rules of the Society.

Earlier pictures from the 1920s to 1940s are in black & white – and include fascinating (for some) contemporary views of the pitch dark conditions in the now disused tunnel down to Ramsgate Harbour, closed in 1926. Shorecliffe Tunnel on the coastal line near Dover is well known for its arched entrances, but your Reviewer has to say that, from within, there seems little to distinguish it from Romsey or even Clayton Tunnels, to take examples from the former South Western and Brighton systems. Sharpthorne Tunnel is now a part of the planned extension of the Bluebell Railway, but the reader is literally left in the dark about this development, the caption referring only to drainage works in the early 1950s.

Interior views are provided, explains the introduction, because most enthusiasts have already seen enough photographs of portals, usually with trains rushing out, but the essence of the tunnel is the interior, the underground experience, the feeling of being cut off from the sunlight. This feeling is indeed well portrayed, the only problem being a certain sameness about the resulting illustrations. (It is also hard to tell if any have been repeated or printed back to front.) The captions are informative, describing construction dates and details, any specific geological or construction problems encountered (the problems on the Hastings line are well known of course), lengths and any variations and even some brief notes on services and, where appropriate, closure dates.

The book follows a roughly East to West survey, though for some reason the tunnel on the Dyke branch is covered on page 47 after Sevenoaks, whereas one might have expected it to come in sequence in Chapter 4. The main LSWR Exeter line through Buckhorn Weston Tunnel has been singled, but it would be hard to tell this from the picture on page 86.

A special chapter at the end covers the Waterloo & City, that BR owned Underground anomaly. However the photographic survey from the southern terminus onwards was made during a power supply failure so it is hard to tell where Waterloo ends and the City begins. A brief note attached to the Introduction on page 5 explains why the Channel Tunnel and other tunnels on the High Speed line have not been included, as a modern construction entirely of concrete segments was never part of the Southern system despite its geographic location.

Perhaps this album is best described as a coffee table book – for the connoisseur of black coffee. Nevertheless, this Reviewer feels it can be recommended to all enthusiasts with tunnel vision. At over £25, one might consider the price a little steep for a book comprising mainly squares of glossy black, but the serious collector should not find this off putting. It doesn't actually fill a black hole in railway publishing, instead it illustrates the black hole. But with gritty and scholarly authenticity.

We understand that a companion volume on the LNER is already under preparation, working from Gasworks Tunnel northwards through the Northern Heights (though why not starting with the Hotel Curve from the Widened Lines?), Potters Bar, Stoke and beyond. Maybe something to fill the hole in that next Christmas stocking?

Available from the Publications Officer, RTHS, Tunnel Cottages, Woodhead, Derbyshire

Walter Rothschild

One for the LMS edition? Or does it let in too much light? Looking north out of Blea Moor Tunnel, towards Dent.
(D Ibbotson)